STEADY-STATE, ZERO GROWTH
AND THE
ACADEMIC LIBRARY

STEADY-STATE, ZERO GROWTH

AND THE

ACADEMIC LIBRARY

a collection of essays
edited by

COLIN STEELE
Deputy Librarian, Australian National University

CLIVE BINGLEY
LONDON

LINNET BOOKS
HAMDEN · CONN

FIRST PUBLISHED IN 1978 BY CLIVE BINGLEY LTD
16 PEMBRIDGE ROAD LONDON W11 UK
SIMULTANEOUSLY PUBLISHED IN THE USA BY LINNET BOOKS
AN IMPRINT OF THE SHOE STRING PRESS INC
995 SHERMAN AVENUE HAMDEN CONNECTICUT 06514
SET IN 10 ON 12 POINT PRESS ROMAN BY ALLSET
PRINTED IN THE UK BY REDWOOD BURN LTD
TROWBRIDGE AND ESHER
COPYRIGHT ©CLIVE BINGLEY LTD 1978
ALL RIGHTS RESERVED
BINGLEY ISBN: 0-85157-243-X
LINNET ISBN: 0-208-01680-5

Library of Congress Cataloging in Publication Data

Main entry under title:

Steady-state, zero-growth and the academic library

    Includes bibliographical references.
    1. Libraries, University and college—
Administration—Addresses, essays, lectures.
I. Steele, Colin.
Z675.U5S74   025.1   78-7030
ISBN 0-208-01680-5

CONTENTS

When we mean to build,
we first survey the plot, then draw the model;
and when we see the figure of the house,
then we must rate the cost of the erection;
which if we find outweighs ability,
what do we then but draw anew the model
in fewer offices, or at least desist
to build at all?

Henry IV Part 2 Act I Scene iii

INTRODUCTION
Colin Steele

The problems may have started with inflation, and may still have a
lot to do with inflation, but the cuts which are going to hurt most in
the next two to three years are directly related to the screwing-down
by the government, for economic and political reasons, of the expansion
of higher education. The result in my opinion is that this country is
now well on the road to becoming a kind of backwater, intellectually
and academically, starved of all sorts of research facilities, including
library materials. (1)

The fact is, libraries can no longer afford to maintain the collections,
staffs, and service levels that librarians and users have come to expect
in the last two decades. Libraries are experiencing a substantial loss
in their standard of living as a result of inflation, increasing energy costs
and changing priorities in our society. We can rail against it and search
for scapegoats, but it would be better if we came to terms with the
painful reality and began to reduce our excessive commitments and
expectations to match our declining resources. (2)

THESE TWO STATEMENTS, by James Thompson and Richard de Gennaro, librarians of Reading and Pennsylvania Universities respectively,
provide a fitting if somewhat sobering backdrop to this volume. Thompson
sees the ultimate result of British government policy in the mid-1970s
as ensuring that British university libraries become undergraduate textbook
factories, with research only possible, particularly in the social sciences
and humanities, at the increasingly powerful sections of the British Library.
This he cannot accept on intellectual or economic grounds. De Gennaro,
on the other hand, in his article and in his remarks at the 1977 conference
of the American Library Association, clearly sees that 'the role of most
academic libraries should be changed to serve as an adjunct to the teaching

7

function of the college or university rather than to researchers except in a small number of institutions where genuine research is actually carried out'. (3)

It is the intention of this volume to explore in broad terms the current state of this debate, and to examine the nature of the events which have led to the situation summarised in the two quotations. The geographical focus is the United Kingdom, for this is where economic cutbacks have been legitimised or, some would argue, bastardised, into an official philosophy of action on the basis of the 1976 Atkinson Report. (4) To a lesser extent Australia is also concerned, because with its close educational links with the United Kingdom it could face similar promulgations if government cutbacks on higher education continue.

The essays in this book do not offer any radical solutions to the present problems facing academic libraries. It would be unrealistic to expect otherwise. They do highlight, however, the urgent need for more research into library operations in all aspects. Until such research is carried out, decisions by governments may well be no more than instinctive reactions to prevailing pressures. Librarians, moreover, cannot argue on effective use of resources, both individually or collectively, if they have no coherent concept of how their libraries are used. The setting up in 1977 of a British University Grants Committee steering group on library research under Dr Anne Whiteman, Vice-Principal of Lady Margaret Hall, Oxford, is a welcome sign. It will be interesting to compare its results and investigations with those emanating from the research team working under Steph Salmon, Assistant Vice-President, Library Planning and Policy, which is investigating the University of California library system.

Some of the large number of topics needing further research were discussed at a seminar at Loughborough University in March 1977. The proceedings have been published as *The future of library collections*. (5) Elizabeth Watson's opening essay in this book also clearly indicates that many of the operations within a library are based more on assumption than hard fact or the evidence produced by careful analysis and costing. Her essay provides basic exploration of the terminology of the debate, be it steady-state, zero-growth, or self-renewing libraries.

Norman Higham in his essay lucidly provides the literature background to the build-up and aftermath of the publication of the Atkinson Report. Two key individuals in the debate both before and after publication were Dr Donald Urquhart and Maurice Line, former and present Directors of the British Library Lending Division at Boston Spa. With Sir Frederick Dainton as Chairman of the University Grants Committee and at the same time President of the Library Association in 1977, it might have been felt that a conflict of interests could ensue. Thus when, in the year of writing, the current Minister of the Arts in the United Kingdom, Lord Donaldson, can speak of 'death rates' and 'destruction' with reference to library collections one can sympathise with those librarians who might feel a lack of friends in high places. (6)

Librarians in time of economic hardship need to be more effective managers and propagandists. As Peter Durey points out in his essay, most library budgets are almost wholly expended on staff and book/serial costs. There is little room to negotiate in order to make savings either within these areas or without. The enactment of such economies usually brings down the wrath of students (angry at reduced opening hours), academics (faced with diminishing purchases of new books and serials) and unions (confronted with staff retrenchments or freezing of posts), if not indeed a combination of all three. Times of economic recession also make negotiations with university budget administrators more difficult as the library's needs cannot be as easily satisfied as other sections of the university—the gap between available hard cash and spiralling book and serial inflation becomes increasingly difficult to close. It is in this area that the librarian, who in any case is often required to be a combination of academic, administrator and computer expert, needs to become an effective lobbyist as well.

Professor Gordon Greenwood of Queensland University in a long and stimulating article, 'Policy formation and library experimentation in Australia and other western societies' (7) brings out the essential fact that, in general, librarians have been far too self-contained in the past, and that they will need to 'sell' their libraries as cost-effective units far more in the future. Greenwood's essay appears in a volume *Design for diversity*, which is the most authoritative yet to appear on libraries and higher education in Australia. The blurb to it announces that 'tertiary education in Australia is a major growth industry'. The events of 1977 however, painfully outdate these words. This was the year in which the Australian Liberal government significantly reduced, in real terms, the funds available for universities.

John Horacek's essay sketches the development of Australian libraries in the context of the physical nature of the continent and its historical evolution. It cannot be stressed too often that the transfer of Atkinsonian concepts to Australia is just not feasible in these contexts, even though it may be attempted.

John Dean's essay picks up and amplifies some of the points Elizabeth Watson raised, and like the other essays poses more questions than we as

9

yet have answers. The work Dean and his colleagues are undertaking under David Stam at Johns Hopkins University, particularly with reference to binding and preservation, will have relevance to many libraries throughout the world. It should, of course, be remembered that the space problem may well solve itself in the twenty-first century, given the extremely poor paper quality of many of the books in collections today. Libraries may well self-destruct of their own accord rather than as a result of some governmental edict. Thus Fraser G Poole, Assistant Director for a Preservation at the Library of Congress told a planning conference for a national preservation program held there in December 1976, that in 1971 the Library of Congress estimated that six million of its seventeen million books were in an advanced state of deterioration. (8)

Bernard Naylor's essay follows on from John Dean's concern with weeding and stock control with particular relevance to individual libraries with an exploration, through the terms of autonomy, costs, information, protocols and machinery, of the bases for future cooperation. In this context it is interesting to see a school of thought emerging, as exemplified b de Gennaro, which argues that regional resource sharing in the long run does *not* save significant amounts of funds. To these writers 'cooperation is merely a pooling of poverty' with the future being with national centres. (9) Such centres will provide access to little used research material and be linked by or control an increasingly sophisticated automated national bibliographical network. (10) In the United States the development of such embryonic networks and the actual establishment of co-operative consortia, such as between Stanford and Berkeley in the west, and New York Public, Yale, Harvard and Columbia in the east, have been aided by grants from 'interested' foundations, particularly the Andrew W Mellon Foundation.

In the United Kingdom and Australia there are no such enlightened foundations. In the former country the role and influence of the British Library has become increasingly dominant, while in the latter much progress remains to be made in either regional or national cooperation. Other writers, particularly Stephen Green in his essay, have commented on the British Library and its present role in the United Kingdom. It seemed fitting to end the volume with his essay on national libraries. In its present form the British Library is quintessentially a product of the 1970s and is a firm indication of future patterns of centralisation and standardisation, both nationally and internationally. The old independence of the individual library and librarians has gone for ever but it is hoped that the other message emerging from this volume is that there still must

10

be room for local initiatives and worthwhile collections within the overall frameworks. If the administrators are too autocratic and centralist, the leaves of the library tree may well begin to wither and die, with all that implies in the future for the profession and the community it serves.

REFERENCES

1 James Thompson in *Coping with cuts. A conference to examine the problems facing academic libraries in the late 1970s* London, National Book League, 1977, 7.

2 Richard de Gennaro 'Copyright, resource sharing and hard times: a view from the field' *American libraries* September 1977, 435.

3 Richard de Gennaro 'Adjusting services to needs and resources' quoted in *Library of Congress information bulletin* July 29 1977, 519.

4 University Grants Committee *Capital provision for university libraries: report of a working party* London, HMSO, 1976. This committee was chaired by Professor R J C Atkinson.

5 J W Blackwood (ed) *The future of library collections* Loughborough, 1977. (L M R U report no 7).

6 Lord Donaldson, speech to ASLIB quoted in *Library Association record* 79(7), July 1977, 345.

7 Harrison Bryan and Gordon Greenwood (eds) *Design for diversity: library services for higher education and research in Australia* St Lucia, University of Queensland Press, 1977, 537-641.

8 Quoted in *Library of Congress information bulletin* 36(7), February 1977, 129.

9 Richard de Gennaro, 'Copyright, resource sharing and hard times' 434.

10 See the papers outlining the progress and the problems in developing such a concept in *Journal of library automation* June 1977, passim; and also H D Avram and L S Maruyama (eds) *Towards a national library and information service network* Library of Congress Network Advisory Group, Washington, Library of Congress, 1977.

THE CONCEPT OF THE STEADY-STATE LIBRARY—
WHOSE DEFINITION?

Elizabeth A Watson

A problem and a solution

THE CONCEPT of the steady-state library attempts to resolve three basic
dilemmas currently confronting academic libraries and the funding bodies
which support their development—the need to cut costs, the need to place
some limits on the indefinite expansion of academic libraries, and the
need to improve performance rates (that is, the ability of libraries to provide, quickly and easily, the material their patrons require). These problems have not come upon us suddenly, they have been in evidence for
some time, but the concept of the steady-state library as a solution to
these problems might have been ignored or remained an academic debate
had not economic pressures become so overwhelming.

No one can ignore the reality of present economic conditions nor the
consequences for institutions of higher education, including academic
libraries, of cutbacks in government expenditure. But not all are in agreement about how academic libraries should respond or should be made to
respond to a situation of no growth or even decline. Some of the disagreement may reflect whether or not the protagonists view the present
financial crisis as just that or as a long-term economic trend. Yet is is
probably true to say that most librarians would accept that even were
present economic circumstances more congenial libraries will need to cut
costs, will need to set limits to their overall size, will need to improve
access to their resources, and that they must face these problems now.

But it is not just librarians who have a say in the definition of the problem. There are politicians and economists, there are members of funding
bodies and university councils, there are academic researchers and teachers;
we may even come to hear a student view of the problem. Any one of
these groups might present the problem in a rather different guise which
would reflect its own value position and its own interests. The solutions
they propose will also reflect those values and interests, which may not be
the values and interests of academic librarians (or of academic patrons).

13

Evolution of a concept

The history of the concept of the steady-state library is not a long one but its development reflects a significant shift away from the values espoused by librarians to those stressed by funding bodies and politicians. The earliest discussions were conducted by librarians and others who have undertaken research in libraries (and with library users being permitted some small part). The most significant development though has come from another source and reflects the interests of groups other than university librarians. In April 1976, the (UK) University Grants Committee released the report of its Working Party on Capital Provision for Libraries (the Atkinson Report). This report and the debate that has followed its publication have ensured that the concept of the steady-state library can never again be simply a topic for debate among librarians or a descriptive term for an experiment which a few academic libraries have engaged in. Since Atkinson it has become a standard, a policy, and a rationale for resource allocation.

It is interesting to reflect how the concept might have evolved had this development not taken place. It is probable that the debate would have widened and deepened and allowed for a more thorough appraisal, not only of the implications but of the underlying assumptions, and the changes in assumptions involved in the adoption of a steady-state solution to the problem of library growth.

The impetus for the earlier debate came from a recognition that, despite claims to the contrary, many librarians still secretly clung to the ideal of self-sufficiency, at least within selected subject areas. An era of unprecedented growth in libraries had allowed that mentality to continue to direct and mould development, even whilst ever-expanding collections failed to keep pace with the publications offered year by year, and even whilst libraries fell further behind in their attempts to supply the greater proportion of their users' needs.

On the other hand, the impetus behind the UGC working party's discussions and recommendations is the immediate and pressing need to cut capital expenditure in tertiary education, and as library space is among the most expensive it is hardly surprising that libraries should be singled out for the (not entirely undivided) attention of the UGC. In casting around for some conceptual framework or rationale for their new standards, the working party lighted upon the notion of a 'no-growth' library, already a well-developed concept with its own literature and its own dedicated body of disciples. They applied the only slightly more satisfactory description 'self-renewing library of limited

14

growth', and developed their own formulae for putting that concept into effect.

What often happens when a government or semi-government authority takes specific action about a so-called problem, is that debate about that problem is circumscribed by the need to respond immediately to specific features of the government initiative. While it is extremely important that there be a thorough airing of what the profession considers both inequitable and absurd in the Atkinson recommendations, there is a considerable risk that a debate about a very significant planning concept will become propelled by these considerations alone. It is important that the kind of debate that does take place is one that opens up and probes those very areas which were overlooked or avoided by the Atkinson Committee, or, to put it another way, the kind of discussion which the UGC by its haste and lack of prior consultation did not allow to take place. (1)

The value of a historical perspective

This is the briefest of histories and a slanted one, but the value of such a perspective is that it shows where we have come from and, perhaps, where we might go. A fuller account would show more clearly what changes in emphasis and direction have taken place and whether there have been changes in the definition of the problem for which the concept steady-state has been devised as a solution. It should indicate why these changes have taken place and who or what groups, what authorities, what experts, what vested interests have had a part in the shaping of the concept. It should also reveal which of these groups have had the most significant impact, which retains the greater hold upon the debate surrounding the concept, and which have the power to define and implement the concept in their own terms. And, according to the value position espoused by the person engaging in the appraisal, these developments can more readily be described as a 'good' or 'necessary' thing, or as 'unfortunate', or as 'disastrous'. And the future of the concept may be more clearly assessed—the possibility of redefinition, of directing the debate along particular lines and developing the concept in terms more acceptable to (most) librarians and users.

I myself take a middle-of-the-road stance and view the progress made to date as unfortunate. This particular value position does not view the application of the concept, as presently defined, as an absolute disaster. It was inevitable that some action had to be taken to bring library development within the constraints of an era of 'no-growth' or even decline. It is also inevitable that the result of such action will be difficult to live with in its initial phases. Nor, clearly, can it be applied universally, at least in

15

its present UGC form, without damaging irreparably the library collections of younger universities, especially those in countries less developed
in library resources than Great Britain or the United States. For all
that, the present notion of a steady state library is not the worst possibl
fate.

But nor is it the best possible compromise. It appears to be based
on some faulty assumptions and others which must still be open to
question. And these are not minor concerns, they are basic to the issue
of the place of a library collection and library personnel in a university
environment. The implications of the introduction of a steady-state
standard are far-reaching. While some of these developments would be
accepted, if not exactly welcomed, by most librarians and users, other
possible developments could not be readily accepted.

Objections to the steady-state library

What are the major objections to the present definition of the steady-
state library? Firstly, that the assumptions on which the concept is
based have been largely unexplored. Even a cursory exploration shows
too many gaps in our understanding of the information requirements
of students and researchers, their use of information, and their behaviou
in libraries and of what libraries can and cannot do in meeting their
clients' information requirements. Secondly, the demands on recurrent
expenditure where we know something about them, and the 'costs' to
our users (and we know very little about these) appear to be excessively
high, and we clearly must know more about both kinds of costs if we
are to plan rationally for the future. Thirdly, that alternative solutions,
planning concepts, rationalisations have not been fully spelt out.

In this chapter I want to look more carefully at each of these objections.

1 Unexplored assumptions
'Mature collections', 'optimum size', 'reasonable size'

Let us begin by examining some of the unexplored assumptions.
The first concerns these three concepts, which have been used extensively in the literature and which are an essential part of that wider
concept, the steady-state library.

The idea of steady-state assumes that there is a point beyond which
libraries ought not to be allowed to grow in overall size, and that this
is not merely an economic necessity but a desirable planning constraint.
Libraries, it is argued, will become more efficient and streamlined, with

their operations geared to providing access to information rather than to the acquisition and processing of more and more materials. (2) The more generally quoted standard defines a 'mature' collection as one which contains eighty to ninety per cent of the titles its patrons wish to see. (3) The research which forms the background to this notion has been directed primarily at establishing core collections and determining what should be weeded to store and what duplicated to improve accessibility. (4) It is not helpful on the question of having to decide upon a point in the development of a particular university when its library may be considered to be satisfying the greater proportion of its patrons' needs. Examination of circulation data and the odd statistics of in-library use can provide at best only a partial measure of the demand on the resources of a particular library. (5) And demand is, of course, determined by the nature of the collection itself. It cannot provide a measure of the extent to which a library is or is not meeting the information requirements of its clientele. If the term 'mature collection' has any significance (and I'm inclined to the view that it's not a very useful term and should be abandoned) then it must surely be judged by some criteria external to the collection itself.

The term 'reasonable size' is used by the Atkinson Report. The standard for resonableness is 'levels of existing practice deemed to be adequate'. (6) The formulae developed are based on what the present situation tells us about the relationship between FTE (full-time equivalent) student numbers and size of libraries. The formulae are presented as a starting point only and allowance is made for future growth, for special collections, and for 'special circumstances', but there is no rationale for the particular measures developed beyond a claim that the members of the working party 'do not think there are any absolute a priori criteria which can be supplied in a situation of this kind'. (7) While that claim is not likely to be disputed, many librarians and academics have been less than happy that the decision as to whether or not new university library buildings should be built will be based on formulae that relate feet of occupied shelving and space for readers to FTE student numbers and produce a universal norm of 1.25 square metres of library space for every planned FTE student.

One would have expected from a working party of some eminence a rather more sophisticated and meaningful basis for the allocation of very limited capital funds. But more than this—if the concept of the steady-state or self-renewing library is to become the planning base for all future library development, and that is what the report proposes,

17

then the concept must have built into it some reasoned notion of that 'certain point' at which it may be argued that a library can and should 'steady' its overall growth. If the steady-state concept is not just a cover-up for huge cutbacks in the capital domain, then it assumes that there are ways of determining when a particular library and its users would be better off with a steady-state library. The concepts of 'mature collection' or 'reasonable size' do not give us that reasoned basis. The first purports to look at the most important variable, that of meeting a proportion of the patrons' demand for books, but its measure is too partial a measure and other factors are ignored. The second is neither a logical construct nor a measure. It is dependent on some unidentified persons' assessment of the adequacy of present conditions. Adequacy is also undefined. The basis for calculation is to be the number of FTE students; the number and the demands of other members of academe are of no account in this particular exercise.

So we turn to the third term, 'optimum size'. Although 'nobody has yet succeeded in defining the "right" collection size for any given set of circumstances', an underlying assumption of the steady-state concept is that such definition is possible. (8) The term 'optimum' suggests that there is a point in a library's growth at which a balance can be achieved between a number of important variables which act in consort or in opposition. 'Optimality' may be a concept that system analysts and operations researchers work with happily, but for librarians and others like them such values are not so readily grasped. In determining the optimum size of libraries, the size at which they can/should be brought into a steady-state condition, the criteria of optimality must be established and ranked in importance and the constraints which operate in each individual setting must also be established. What is sought is not 'the ideal' but the best possible compromise given what we know about such factors as size of collection and costs, size of collection and satisfaction of user information requirements, type of access and storage costs and user preference, proportion of students to teaching staff to research staff and type of collection, type of access and seating provision, and so on. And this must be considered against the background of known constraints such as available resources in the form of budget allocations, land, existing buildings, and other constraints such as location restrictions, political factors, etc.

Clearly, some of these factors are more readily measured than others. There have been a number of attempts to develop micro-economic models for determining the optimum size and minimum costs of a library. (9) There is an ample literature concerning the diminishing returns for users as a library increases the number of titles acquired and retains titles indefinitely. (10) And there is a growing concern to establish at what point dis-economies of scale come into play. (11) In many areas we have almost no 'objective' data and we must look at these areas and incorporate them in our research programmes. We must develop means of measuring some of those significant variables that have long been accepted as not amenable to measurement.

If we accept, as it appears that most librarians and users do, that there must be a limit to library expansion, then we must look for the soundest procedures for determining that limit—procedures that make sound economic sense, which protect the integrity of collections and which look to the patrons' requirements for quick and easy access to information. No arbitrary formula can ensure that all these factors are taken into account even when it is proposed as only a starting point. And a steady-state concept that incorporates such arbitrary formulae is of very questionable value as a planning concept.

'Weeding' and use criteria

The second set of assumptions underlying the present definition of steady-state libraries concerns 'weeding' of the collection and the application of 'use' criteria. It is not clear how librarians are to go about weeding their collections to the extent that a steady-state concept implies. If one is to remove to store a volume of material approaching the volume of new accessions the assumption must be that relegation and retirement programmes have become as significant a part of library operations as the acquiring and processing of new materials. The assumption is also that relegation on so massive a scale must, to be viable, employ formulae across the board and wherever possible make use of automated systems. If these are the assumptions on which a steady-state library is to operate then a number of important queries must be raised.

The first concerns the criteria which are to be used in relegation. Clearly qualitative formulae cannot be used for the massive programme the steady-state library implies. What will need to be applied are quantitative formulae that employ measures of use, and that means past circulation. Though few would disagree that use criteria should be part of any assessment of what should be relegated, many users and librarians do not agree, as much of the American literature assumes, that weeding can be carried out with the application of such use criteria alone. While past use may be the best predictor of future use and in-library use figures may correlate significantly with circulation figures, when it comes to applying these criteria to individual books the problems can be enormous and the solutions extremely costly. It is not an easy matter to predict the 'useful book'. The size of the weeding programme and the dependence on use criteria ensure that libraries will, more and more, purchase and retain what is in demand. This can only have a detrimental effect on the quality not only of research collections but, some would argue, of undergraduate collections as well. 'A library rigorously selected for its current utility puts blinders on students and diminishes opportunity for him to strike out on his own'. (12)

We need to know more about use criteria, about in-library use, about what material is more typically used within the library and that which is more likely to be borrowed, about what factors affect use statistics and how they may be manipulated, about quality and extent of use as distinct from number of times borrowed. We need to experiment with other means of determining the value of material from the user point of view. If a library employs a bar code system with its automated circulation system, bar code readers could be installed on each floor of a library and patrons invited to use them to record not only that they have used a particular book in the library but whether they judge the book useful or worthless or some other more specific evaluation. The light pen would be passed over both the bar code of the book and the relevant judgement. (13)

The second query about the massive weeding programmes of the steady-state library concerns the treatment of different disciplinary areas. It seems to be assumed that the application of use criteria will ensure that there will be no 'discrimination' against any particular discipline. Critics of the steady-state concept claim, however, that we know enough about the different rates of obsolescence of scientific literature on the one hand and of the humanities on the other to conclude that removal of thirty per cent (Gore's formula) of a scientific collection would produce a very different effect upon the integrity of that collection from the effect produced upon a humanities collection if a similar percentage were removed. We are also beginning to see that 'the phenomenon (of "obsolescence") is much more complex than has been stated in the past, and that a simple exponential model must be treated with extreme caution'. (14)

The third query concerns the implications of steady-state relegation programmes for all other aspects of library organisation. Unless the steady-state concept is more fully developed and the implications

20

for accessions policies, for the reference function, for the development of the catalogue, for reader education and so on, are spelt out, then the concept has very limited value, as a planning concept, as a new strategy for libraries. Without this wider definition, the concept must be viewed as a convenient catchphrase, a way of dressing up a programme of massive cut backs in capital spending on libraries. The earlier debate in the USA had begun to explore this wider picture even if in very general and rather rosy terms. The recent debate has, by and large, ignored these important considerations.

The user and his response to the steady-state library

To the assumptions concerning optimality and weeding must be added a third assumption or set of assumptions. These concern the academic library user and his response to the steady-state library. Two of these assumptions are of particular importance. The first is that users are not deprived or inconvenienced provided they obtain specific material within a reasonable time. The second is that a smaller, up-to-date, utilitarian collection facilitates efficient use, that the user is not hindered by shelves 'cluttered' with material which is esoteric or highly specialised and consequently little in demand.

The first of these assumptions raises two specific issues; the place of browsing and the importance of quick delivery of materials. The latter question may be more readily investigated and some attempt has already been made to establish how important it is to have material straightaway. (15) Librarians have tended to assume that time is of the essence, but for some categories of users this may not be so and a steady-state library with its local store and access to a vast repository may be little handicap to certain users. What needs to be studied is the effect on users of any kind of barrier to material they want or think they want. If material is not immediately available how many users take the line of least resistance and forget it, or put the reference aside in a card file, or look for another book? Is this a question primarily of time, or laziness, or of lack of organisation, or something else?

The importance of browsing is a more delicate issue. It is clear that many who scornfully reject the browsing argument have defined browsing very narrowly and in so doing have predetermined the judgement that must be made of browsing behaviour. Dr D J Urquhart, for example, whose contempt for browsing is well-known, sees the term as applying only to 'the accidental stumbling across something of interest'. (16) He claims that it is 'not clear to what extent browsing results from the absence of suitable bibliographies, or ignorance about bibliographies, or

intellectual laziness'. (17) He views browsing as an activity which made
sense in the seventeenth century 'when the total volume of publication
was much smaller than it is today and when there were few bibliograph
amd may still be 'a useful activity for an undergraduate who does not
know what he wants but who must have a book immediately'. (18) Hi
faith in bibliographies and such directories seems absolute. Perhaps in
his own field bibliographies are sufficiently numerous, wide-ranging and
biased in ways he approves for him to have such confidence in them.
But it is definitely not the case in many other areas, perhaps in *most*
other areas. Have we really examined the coverage given by bibliographical works? Have we looked at their biases and their deficiencies
and sought an evaluation of them by the academics for whom, presumably, they were compiled? Do we have any understanding of the peculi
problems faced by those working in interdisciplinary areas? (And let us
remember that the interdisciplinary persepective, if we may call it such,
has permeated all academic study to a greater or lesser degree.)

The whole question of browsing needs careful examination. It is
clear that most academics engage in browsing of one kind or another
quite frequently and that they value and enjoy the experience. (19)
What we do not know is whether the value gained from such activity
is sufficiently great to warrant retention of a higher proportion of little
used material on open access than the present definition of steady-state
would seem to countenance. It is again a question of user benefits/
disbenefits against the cost of providing a particular kind of access to
materials; in this case the costs of space for open access provision
against staff costs in maintaining closed store accommodation. To
examine this kind of 'playing-off' of various forces will take more than
a 'how-do-you-browse-and-when-and-why' questionnaire study. (20)

The second important assumption about the users' response to the
steady-state library is that the academic patron, whether student,
teacher, or researcher, will be aided in his use of the library by the
removal to store of not merely out-dated and obsolete material but also
of highly specialised or esoteric works which are rarely borrowed. Yet
there is no evidence to date that patrons are actually hindered in their
use of the library by the presence of lesser-used material on the shelves.
Certainly out-dated or obsolete material (although let us proceed with
care in this area) is best removed. Quite apart from space consideration
users, in most instances, want up-to-date material, not superseded accounts. Obsolete material may be considered 'clutter' but where is the

evidence that removal of thirty per cent of a collection, as Gore advocates, will enhance that collection's appeal and 'usability'? All that can be claimed is that if more space can be made available in open access areas there will be more room to house duplicate copies of works in high demand and this together with the swing to immediate demand criteria in the acquisition of library materials will greatly improve accessibility to works in high demand. But this is a very different claim and must be treated as such.

The unexplored assumptions which are discussed here do not, of course, constitute an exhaustive list. The assumptions are basically of two kinds. Assumptions about patterns of use in university libraries and user information requirements ('philosophical') and assumptions of an organisational, management or costing nature ('technical'). We have dealt primarily with the former kind. Among the more technical assumptions those concerning cost are, as mentioned earlier, a major area of contention and should be dealt with separately.

2 The question of costs

The question of costs is central to the concept of the steady-state library. The term steady-state is, of course, a borrowed term. It has been used extensively by engineers to describe man-made systems where inputs and outputs are adjusted so as to maintain a state of equilibrium, and in astronomy to describe a particular theory about the origins and nature of the universe. In neither context is the question of costs a feature of the steady-state concept. But as a term in librarianship its use is much more recent and its development has resulted almost solely from economic considerations. As was mentioned briefly at the beginning of the chapter, the introduction of the term or one of its synonyms to describe a new notion of library development came at the end of a period of unprecedented growth and expansion for university libraries, particularly in the USA. By the beginning of the seventies, the need for a reappraisal of the development goals of university libraries had become urgent. If university libraries had not been able during a period of uncharacteristic affluence to keep pace with new developments in university teaching and research programmes, how much more pressed would they find themselves in a period of no-growth or even decline? (21) Although the stress in the early debate was on the impracticality and undesirability of indefinite expansion, the context for the debate and the continuing thrust behind the development of the concept have been changing economic circumstances.

At this point in the debate it is clear that most librarians and academic have accepted the impracticality and even the undesirability of indefinite expansion. And most would agree that in the short term, the application of the steady-state concept as a planning tool would bring about considerable capital savings. But two areas remain quite unclear. The first is the area of the recurrent costs of operating steady-state libraries. The second concerns those more elusive costs not readily amenable to measurement, the costs to patrons of university libraries if the future development of their libraries is to be on a steady-state basis.

Recurrent costs

The crux of the recurrent costs issue is the increased staffing costs involved in operating a steady-state library efficiently. Automation may greatly assist in 'weeding' and in expensive record-changing tasks, but the massive relegation programmes implicit in the steady-state concept will require a whole new staffing division within university libraries. And if automation can take over many of the routine and clerical areas, the need for expensive professional staff remains. Professional judgement will be all the more important if circulation data on their own are not considered a sufficient basis for relegation and, for example, professional scrutiny of lists produced by automated circulation systems is required. Apart from the weeding programmes, the storage schemes will require extra staff for removing material to a store, receiving and processing requests for stored material and delivering it to the main library. Stored material will also need to be weeded. Extra staff require extra space. All these costs are continuing costs. Critics of the recommendations of the Atkinson Committee point out that if long-term costs far outweight short-term capital savings, it is difficult to see how such a situation could long be tolerated by universities and funding bodies which consider that libraries already consume an excessively high proportion of recurrent funds.

To appreciate the extent of the recurrent commitment necessitated by steady-state we will need more information. As yet we have little conclusively valid and reliable data on the costs of alternative methods of 'weeding' collections, alternative methods of storage, different methods of organising library collections. Without such information it is difficult to begin to make the judgements which the steady-state concept, as a planning concept, presupposes. In addition, we must be prepared to undertake detailed cost analyses of each alternative plan for future library development (within the overall steady-state framework) in each unique university environment. What may make economic sense in one environment may be nonsense in another. The picture we need is one in which all important variables are taken into account—availability and cost of

24

university land and competing demands for it, off-campus storage availability and cost of rent, cost of building and maintenance of off-campus
storage, cost of providing a certain proportion of a collection on open
access against a proportion in closed stack against a proportion in storage,
the costs associated with possible alternative locations, costs of centralised as against de-centralised systems, cost of using inter-library loans
(ILL) as against acquiring certain books, what proportion of user demand might be sustained economicallly through ILL rather than through
acquisition, and the influence of such decisions on overall growth and
space requirements in the immediate future.

This is the only way to ensure that very limited capital funds are wisely
spent. No funding body has the time to undertake this kind of costing
exercise. It will have to be done by librarians themselves, drawing on
expertise in the costing field. If this is not done then the sort of formulae
that the Atkinson Committee devised may be the alternative we have to
contend with. It is worth remembering that even without the Atkinson
Committee and the steady-state concept, librarians would have been forced
not only to be more cost-conscious but to be much more sophisticated in
their handling of financial matters, and much more at ease with costing
models and with attempts to measure the inputs and outputs of libraries.

Costs to library users

Modelling of this kind is a demanding exercise. It is dependent upon
the development of effective measures of the important cost variables.
The measurement of user benefits and disbenefits will almost certainly
prove the most difficult cost area to deal with. Yet if costing models are
to be devised which attempt to evaluate the cost-effectiveness of long-
term library planning alternatives they must include such variables. They
must attempt to balance, on the one hand, the cost to users of delays in
receiving material, loss of immediate access to certain materials, lessened
browsing opportunities, and on the other hand, increased access to high
demand material and more streamlined services and all of these against the
other more palpable costs of land, buildings, different uses of space, automation, staffing costs, delivery costs. A daunting task.

Much of the research that will be necessary if we are to develop these
more elaborate costing models will need to be undertaken whether or not
steady-state libraries become the norm and whether or not the present
financial crisis is to be a continuing one.

3 Alternatives to steady-state and necessary complementary action

Before commenting further on research priorities, a third major area
of contention must be briefly mentioned. The kind of debate that has

developed since the publication of the Atkinson Report has pre-empted discussion of other options, of alternative 'solutions', alternative planning concepts, courses of action and needed reform in related areas. These need to be spelt out either as alternatives to the steady-state concept or as necessary complementary action if something like the steady-state library comes to be accepted as the basis for all future academic library development. As it would require several volumes to explore the issues in any detail we must content ourselves with only a few isolated commen. The literature to date has been sparse but a few areas emerge. Two of the most significant relate to the two 'information cycles' in which the library is involved—the ' "publication cycle" of production of new knowledge, its formalisation and its storage and use; and a "demand cycle" ' of attempti to meet the demands made on a library for materials which its patrons require. (22)

The 'demand cycle'

In recent years we have heard more and more university librarians calling on their own institutions and on universities at large to look afresh at the process by which new research and teaching programmes are implemented and the way in which such decisions 'involve a library factor, with cost and lead-time components'. (23) Research programmes require libra resources, some require a great deal of library material. 'The cost of acquiring and organising a collection sufficient for even the smallest research project is very large in time as well as money'. (24) All such collections 'have a low probability of continuing use'. (25)

The argument that librarians are propounding is that these resources should be viewed as an investment not an overhead cost and the probability of use must be increased. This can be done in a number of ways. On the one hand, libraries can attempt to ensure that the resources are made available to the largest possible community of researchers. On the other hand, universities should ensure that research interests once established are continued and not allowed to drop when a particular academic moves on. (26) The alternative would be to move the resources where the continued research interest exists. There should also be a rationalisation of the decisions which lead to the establishment of these costly resources in the first instance. (27) When recruiting research staff, university authorities or recruitment boards should discuss with each applica the available resources in his area. They should 'test the match of interest and potential, and of available resources and budget; and having accepted the match, reconcile themselves to such limits'. (28) Researchers should encouraged to explore available but underused resources. Where a

26

researcher can claim no adequate resources exist in any institution for research in a new and significant area, then a university council might give consideration to whether it is prepared to undertake a long-term commitment in that area and provide for a continuing library investment in a new research field. Researchers must become reconciled to the fact that their 'right' to do research must be constrained by questions of cost in the area of library provision. The call for rationalisation recognises that rationalisation must occur both within and among institutions and also inter-institutionally within any given discipline. (29)

The 'publication cycle'

In the 'publication cycle' the library has again been caught-up in a demand cycle over which it has little control. But academic libraries are beginning to look more closely at this demand and to question some of the processes by which they acquire new publications. Henry Voos in an article entitle 'The information explosion; or, redundancy reduces the charge!', discusses the way in which redundancy contributes heavily to the literature explosion. (30) Like other researchers in this area he questions the use of a term like 'information explosion'. If anything it is a 'paper explosion' and the term 'explosion' is not a very apt description of a phenomenon that has been going on for several decades. He discusses the enormous costs involved in the multiple indexing of the same material in different indexes and in different ways. This is particularly apparent in the coverage of technical reports. Other forms of redundancy are also apparent and these are of more immediate concern to acquisition librarians. The first is the republication in book form of articles previously available as either journal articles or technical reports. The second is the republication of the writings of a single author.

The recommendations with which Voos concludes his article are reforms which must be implemented by organisations other than libraries but the result would be a considerable saving to libraries. These reforms would also bring about savings to users in time wasted 'culling through indexes for material which might be relevant, but which has already been scanned by him without him being aware of it'. (31)

If the steady-state concept is addressed to the need to cut library costs, to examine the demand for more and more space to house collections and also to the need to improve access to library resources, then the two areas discussed above must be seen as being of the same vital importance in an overall plan to rationalise the provision of library support for study, teaching and research in universities.

Action libraries must take

Other areas are more the immediate responsibility of libraries. All
academic libraries should begin to implement 'collection review' programmes with a thorough reappraisal of acquisition policies and the
expansion of weeding programmes so as to forestall some of the pressing demands on open access space. Libraries must increase their efforts
in areas which will in themselves help reduce recurrent expenditure or
at least help to keep a check on recurrent costs. These include the use
of automated systems in collection weeding programmes especially in the
altering of documents, the development of the kinds of networks which
facilitate the rationalisation of cataloguing processes, acquisition policie
and resource sharing and the investigation of ways of reorganising and
upgrading ILL systems.

Research and its place in the scheme of things

Finally, among these other necessary courses of action is research,
particularly research which looks at the communities we serve and their
need for a certain kind of library service. This, of course, is not an
alternative course of action in the way that rationalisation of university research programmes or the reduction of duplication in indexes.
and abstracting journals might be said to be. A major criticism of the
steady-state concept particularly its embodiment in the recommendatio
of the Atkinson Committee is the inadequate data on which it is based
The briefest examination of underlying assumptions makes apparent
the paucity of information we possess about questions of central conce
The area of costs is an obvious one but the area of user behaviour and
information needs is, I believe, an area of ever greater importance. We
need to win support for research into user information requirements ar
the place of the library in university research, teaching and study. (32)
If we are to make valid judgements about what services we can dispens
with and what ought to be retained at all cost we need a great deal mo
understanding of our clients and their information needs. We must kno
more about the likely effect of certain choices upon users and their
work. The criticisms of much so called user research to date are well
known. But the 'user component' in all library research requires some
attention. We need to keep in mind the value positions we espouse in
research. Library research is typically inward looking, a library view of
library problems, and although it is not necessarily unaware of the user
he is consulted only in 'library terms' perhaps as a measure of how
efficiently the library is doing what it is doing.

The raison d'être for a university library and the reason for spending
money on a university library is the academic community it serves, and

28

that community's need for access to information sources. This rationale may be lost sight of in a debate which focuses on costs and formulae, weeding procedures and collection integrity, the optimum size for a collection and the economics of book storage and all the theoretical and technical problems to which we have already referred. We must become more client-oriented and more informed about the communities we serve.

Conclusion: statement of a value position

In this chapter, I have examined the concept of the steady-state library as it is now presented to us. I looked briefly at its history and the changes that have taken place both in the definition of the problem to which the concept is addressed and in the concept itself.

There are two assumptions underlying this approach. The first is that the concept of the steady-state library is here to stay; it cannot be ignored or dismissed. The second is that, as concepts of this kind evolve over time, they are open to redirection or redefinition. In the case of the steady-state library concept such redefinition is essential. Further research and experience will make this process clearer than it is at present.

If we accept that university libraries cannot go on growing in overall size indefinitely, and that at some point in their development each library could 'steady' its growth and continue to operate efficiently, economically, and in the best interests of its clients, then we accept that we will be living with some kind of steady-state library. Precisely what that notion of a steady-state library is and how it is to be applied, is the crucial question.

Earlier in the chapter I spoke of adopting a 'middle-of-the-road' value position. This value position accepts the inevitablity of some kind of steady-state solution to the problem of housing library collections in an era of financial constraint, but it has considerable reservations about the present definition of the concept and about its application. While it accepts absolutely the impossibility of self-sufficiency it does envisage libraries continuing to purchase large numbers of books and serials in an effort to keep somewhat abreast of developments in the fields of interest to them. It assumes, however, that there must be much more careful scrutiny of what is purchased and that blanket orders are a thing of the past. But it would strongly resist any pressure to purchase only what has been placed on student reading lists or the few new works by the 'established names' in a particular discipline.

This value position accepts that these expanding collections or the greater part of them cannot continue to be housed in open access libraries or even in large closed or partially closed stack areas. It accepts the increasing use of storage areas and accepts that some of these will be remote from the parent library. It is emphatic about the necessity of back-up facilities in the form of a national or of large regional repositories.

It is a value position that accepts that a large, well-organised weeding programme will become as essential a part of library operations as the acquiring and processing of new books. It accepts that use criteria will need to be applied more rigorously and thoroughly than anything practised in the past. But it demands that as much user response as possible be provided for and that we start experimenting with ways of incorporating user judgements about the worth of books in our weeding procedures It can be done, it must be done.

This value position does not accept the simplistic notions of 'reasonable size' or 'mature collection' that have framed the present definition of steady-state. It does, accept, however, that there can be determined for each library a point at which it can and should 'steady' its overall growth. It argues against the imposition of across-the-board, arbitrary standards that do not take into account the different stages of development, the different areas of specialisation, the different functions in library networks, or in a given city or community, of different kinds of academic libraries. While agreeing that bigger is not necessarily better it would advocate the acceptance of larger on-campus libraries than most steady-state formulations or standards appear to allow. It would dispute that smaller libraries are, especially in research establishments, better libraries.

This value position welcomes the reappraisal of the goals of academic libraries, of their place in university communities. It accepts as long overdue the shift in emphasis from holdings to access, from size to availability but is not ready to accept uncritically the glib use of terms such as 'working collection'.

This in-the-middle position requires a much more demanding and careful costing of the alternative solutions to the problem of housing an expanding collection in each unique environment. It contends that librarians must be responsible for providing costing evidence of this kind.

It is a value position that stresses alternative and additional lines of action in rationalising the use of available resources and in ensuring that future funds are spent in ways that lessen duplications, upgrade services, and increase access.

It emphatically states that the steady-state concept must be redefined and that unless and until further research and experience indicates otherwise the redefinition should be in the terms set out above. Even so redefined it must never be viewed as a panacea for the problems we are facing in this era of the no-growth economy. The steady-state library will itself create special problems that we have yet to resolve or learn to live with; it has implications for other aspects of library organisation (ie other than how and where books are stored) which have yet to be explored and costed; and it has nothing to say about vast areas of possible future library development, cooperation and rationalisation which may have as much to do with the realistic and responsible use of available resources and with offering a better service to our academic clientele.

REFERENCES

1 It should be noted that more recently the UGC has stressed that the 'Atkinson "norms" on the size of university libraries are to be regarded purely as a starting point . . .' and that it has 'set up a series of research studies on library work under a steering group . . .'. See the *Times higher education supplement* April 22 1977.

2 For example Daniel Gore 'Farewell to Alexandria: the theory of the no-growth, high performance library' in *Farewell to Alexandria* New York, Greenwood Press, 1976.

3 Ibid. See also the article on which the above is based 'Zero growth: when is NOT-enough enough? A symposium' *The journal of academic librarianship* 1(5), 1975, 4-11. See particularly Gore's contribution, 4-5, and that of Richard W Trueswell, 6-7.

4 See the work of Richard W Trueswell eg *Analysis of library user circulation requirements, final report* NSF grant GNO 435 (January 1968), and 'User circulation satisfaction vs size of holdings at three academic libraries' *College and research libraries* 30(3), May 1969, 204-213.

5 See R H Orr's excellent article 'Measuring the goodness of library services: a general framework for considering quantitative measures' *Journal of documentation* 29(3), September 1973, 315-332, and especially 324-326.

6 University Grants Committee *Capital provision for university libraries: report of a working party* London, HMSO 1976, 7.

7 Ibid. 7.

8 A Graham Mackenzie 'Whither our academic libraries: a partial view of management research' *Journal of documentation* 32(2), 1976, 131.

9 See eg I A Douglas 'Optimum size of a library of monographs' *Australian library journal* November 1973, 404-407 and D Rowe

'Application of the theory of the firm to library costing' *Australian libra journal* 23(3), April 1974, 108-111.

10 See eg Michael H Buckland *Book availability and the library user* New York, Pergamon, 1975, particularly part two.

11 See eg the comments made by B J Enright in the introduction to J A and N C Urquhart *Relegation and stock control in libraries* Stocksfields, Oriel Press, 1976, 6.

12 Ray L Heffner in 'Zero growth: when is NOT-enough enough?' See reference 3.

13 Obviously there would have to be built-in checks in the system fo recording use. Patrons might be tempted to pass the pen over the bar code of a particular book ten times just to make sure. The system could be designed to accept only one recorded use of a particular volume withi an hour. This suggestion has been made by Tony Ashcroft, Systems Programmer in the Australian National University Library. Its implemen tation is explained along with other suggestions for the deployment of computer equipment in 'Sequential uses for library computer equipment ANU Library Background Paper, (unpublished).

14 Colin F Cayless 'Evaluating administrative effectiveness in librarie *Studies in library management 3* ed Holroyd. London, Bingley, 1976; Hamden, Conn, Linnet, 177. Cayless is referring to the authoritative review of obsolescence by M B Line and A Sandison entitled 'Obsolescence and changes in use of literature with time' *Journal of documentation* 30(3), September 1974, 283-350.

15 See the report of a study of BLLD users by B Houghton and C Prosser 'A survey of the opinions of BLDD users in special libraries of th effects of non-immediate access to journals' *Aslib proceedings* 26(9), 1974, 354-66 and of a study at the University of Lancaster by M Stuart 'Some effect on library users of the delays in supplying publications' *Aslib proceedings* 29(1) 1977, 34-45.

16 In a reply to a letter by Dr E D Whittle of the University of Edinburgh, in the *BLL review* 5(1), 1977, 33.

17 In an article in the *Times higher education supplement* Septembe 17 1976, 8.

18 In an article in the *BLL review* 4(1), 1976, 8, 'National lending/ reference libraries or libraries of first resort'.

19 See eg Francis Celoria 'The archaeology of serendip' *Library journal* May 1 1969, 1846-1848, and the letter from Dr E D Whittle in the *BLL review* 5(1), 1977, 32.

20 A notable start has been made in the study of browsing behaviour by Richard Joseph Hyman *Access to library collections: an inquiry into the validity of the direct shelf approach, with special reference to browsing* Metuchen, N J, Scarecrow Press, 1972. See also Philip M Morse's attempt to quantify browsing behaviour and to use this understanding to establish what size the open access proportion of a collection should be to optimise the success of the average browser 'Search theory and browsing' *Library quarterly* 40(4), October 1970, 391-408.

21 Richard de Gennaro 'Austerity, technology and resource sharing: research libraries face the future' *Library journal* 100(10), 15 May 1975, 917-923.

22 Donald A Redmond, Michael P Sinclair, and Elinore Brown 'University libraries and university research' *College and research libraries* 33(6), November 1972, 447.

23 Ibid, 453.

24 Ibid, 447.

25 Ibid, 448.

26 There will be times when research and teaching programmes would be better shut down and the investment in library resources written off. But it should be a decision taken for clearly stated reasons. A programme should not be allowed to lapse.

27 Ibid, 448.

28 Ibid, 453.

29 Ibid, 452.

30 In *College and research libraries* 32(1), 1971, 7-14.

31 Ibid, 9.

32 The need for a carefully thought out, long term programme of user studies has been recognised by some institutions. A notable example is the new Centre for Research on User Studies at the University of Sheffield, funded by the British Library (R & D Dept). It is disappointing, however, that, at least in its initial statement of objectives and major areas of concern, the centre seems to be entirely caught up with questions of techniques and methods.

THE STATE OF THE ARGUMENT: UNITED KINGDOM

Norman Higham

DISCUSSIONS which have taken place over the years and have accelerated recently, have largely avoided the strict concept of zero-growth. What is at present under discussion is the idea of the 'self-renewing library' defined as 'a library of limited size in which beyond a certain point material should be reduced at a rate related to the rate of acquisition'. The quotation is from the report of the working party set up by the (UK) University Grants Committee under the chairmanship of Professor R J C Atkinson, and published in 1976. (1) And it was the formation of this working party and the publication of its report which caused the acceleration previously mentioned, in discussions on the subject, especially on the part of those university librarians, numerically in the majority, antagonistic to the concept.

It may be asked why these librarians had not previously joined in the debate on the steady-state library, which has engrossed transatlantic librarians over a number of years. A few in fact had done so, but the majority silently pursued their acquisition policies, no doubt in the belief that the dangers of expansion lay far in the future. The comparative book stocks of American and British university libraries offered a basis for reassurance that in this country the size of libraries was not in itself a reason for radical measures. But the increase in the numbers of universities and the decline in the availability of UGC capital funds for building has altered the situation. An argument on principles has been penetrated by that which renders argument superfluous, lack of money. He who would warn the villager in Bangladesh of the dangers of over-eating need not labour the point.

The attention of the University Grants Committee was officially drawn to the problem of expansion in 1967 by the publication of the Parry Report. (2) Parry was cautious on the matter: 'The inevitable expansion of their libraries presents universities with one of their most difficult problems.' The presence of the word 'inevitable' was significant; the

34

steady-state library played no part in their thinking. Indeed even in the steady-state university, or as the report puts it 'even in a numerically static institution, the library will, of course, continue to grow as more and more material of scholarly interest pours off the world's presses'. It points out that British university libraries are small by comparison with some foreign university libraries, particularly American, and quotes from the Standing Conference on National and University Libraries (SCONUL) submission: 'The Association of Research Libraries publishes statistics for sixty-three of its members, and it is particularly significant that if the largest British universities (excluding Oxford, Cambridge and London) were members, they would rank lower than fifty-sixth on the list for size of stock, annual accessions, expenditure on books, periodicals and binding, and cost of staff salaries.'

The report goes on to say that while expansion on the American scale has little to recommend it, the answer to the question of indefinite expansion should not depend on space or funds, but that 'the criterion of growth should be the degree of usefulness to users attained thereby'. However, 'neither space nor funds are likely to be unlimited and that some means must be found of controlling expansion, without damaging the services which university libraries feel it their duty to give to their users'. It thus anticipated the view of the Atkinson Committee with the difference that the latter body was immediately confronted with the limitations foreseen by its predecessor.

The Parry Committee saw some alleviation through the use of microforms, but accepted that library growth would not be appreciably affected thereby, and that withdrawal of stock must be considered. It pointed however to the difficulties, the cost and the dangers of discarding books from research collections, points which were echoed in reactions to the Atkinson Report of 1976.

The report concluded that 'apart from the University of London, which has its own problems, there is as yet no university library in Britain large enough to need a depository. But it becomes evident, when considering essential growth in the next twenty-five years, that some withdrawal of material for deposit will have to be undertaken by university libraries. Criteria for determining the nature of such material will have to be decided.'

By the time of the publication of the Atkinson Report only nine years later, a number of university libraries were already out-housing material on a larger scale than previously. This became necessary because lack of main library space preceded the provision of new buildings or extensions.

It is not to say that the storage of books elsewhere than on open access shelves was new. It is a reasonable guess that most university libraries of any age have had to dump sections of the bookstock in corridors or dista rooms. They have also discarded books, despite the image created that university libraries throw nothing away. But with a very few exceptions relegation to store has not been a large element in library organisation, and discarding has been minimal.

Generally speaking, relegation was seen as a necessary inconvenience users and library staff arising from lack of space. It was not widely considered as a benefit. But a few librarians in this country were taking up the idea of the limited size library. In 1973, Maurice Line ended the chapter ('Local acquisition policies in a national concept') which he con tributed to the festschrift for Joan Gladstone, *The art of the librarian*, with the oft-repeated words, 'In place of the fat bloated libraries of the past, we can expect lean muscular libraries—and they will be all the fitte for that.' (3)

Whether the anthropomorphic imagery really stands up to examinati (one might say in reply that a library need rather the physique of a weig lifter to support university research!), the message was clear. A library more efficiently serve its users if it strips away the unused material whic clutters its shelves. He argues that the pursuit of size had dogged the acquisition policies of university librarians. 'Size has been one of the few measures that can be easily calculated, and unfortunately it has bee used as a measure of value; clearly a far better measure would be the lev of satisfaction of potential demands on the library.'

The basis for Line's argument is the existence of an efficient national lending system providing a back-up service for local needs. At the unde graduate level at least ninety-five per cent of demands should be met by the university library or by the student himself. At the research level the measure is more difficult but it is argued that it should be possible, given appropriate study, to assess potential demand as a guide in decidir whether to purchase or acquire on interloan.

Line cites two examples to illustrate his point: 'At one extreme is th serial which does not cost very much, and for which there are twenty, thirty or more requests a year. At the other extreme is the obscure boo in a foreign language which is of particular interest to one member of st only, for the research he is currently conducting. In the former case, the item should clearly be bought; in the latter case, purchase has bee necessary in the past but will probably not be necessary in the future Between these two extremes, there are many serials that are required

36

few times in the year, and many books requested by one or two re-searchers.'

Some kind of value-judgements about cases like the above are regularly made by those selecting acquisitions. That they are often comparatively crude explains why some acquired books are little-read even when new. The problem is to refine the process, to define the phrase 'does not cost very much', to write into the case of the 'obscure book in a foreign language' the value of the research to be carried out, its duration, the possibility of research students taking it up, and the cost, difficulties and indeed likelihood of borrowing the book from elsewhere.

What Line is advocating is an acquisition policy which takes into account the existence of a comprehensive national collection available for loan or in photocopy. The prerequisite for this is further study into the needs of users and the patterns of their use of libraries. Accompanying this is the prediction of the library of limited size, the lean muscular library.

It could be argued that the difference between the Parry Committee's views and those of Maurice Line was simply one of degree, that both were predicting the need for some restrictions or expansion of libraries. But Maurice Line was concerned to argue that the situation was urgent and that librarians needed to change their attitudes. This had been the view of Donald Urquhart as far back as 1967 speaking at a conference on research into library services in higher education. (4)

It was Urquhart's paper which influenced Brian Enright to change his own attitude, clearly expressed in his chapter in the Urquhart festschrift *Essays on information and libraries*, under the title 'Biblioclothanasia' (a library application of the condition 'oclothanasia: death by overcrowding') (5). His criticism of what he sees as the traditional university library is scathing: 'A librarian who appears to advocate stock control is likely to be branded as an enemy of books, a bibliothecal quisling . . . There is almost a divine right of growth for libraries which appears to make any apology unnecessary and questioning almost barbaric and indecent.' (page 64). He accepts that 'it would clearly be a disaster if the concept of stock control was used (or abused) in a way which weakened libraries and the contribution they can make to the community.' And he further accepts that stock control or 'de-acquisition' would be 'as costly (if not more so) than the process of acquisition itself.' Nevertheless he argues that 'library obesity creates a "negative browsing" situation and an unhelpful collection bias.' He advocates a continuous programme of book retirement: '. . . it seems essential for librarians to become masters of stock control, to set out to establish not as a crash emergency programme but as a normal part

37

of their routine operations a new regimen of library hygiene, the scienc
of bibliothecal health . . . '.

Traditional university librarianship appeared relatively unmoved by
these medical analogies. The literature contains little in the way of rebut
tal of the newly proclaimed doctrines. The principle of continued expan
remained implicit in all writings on acquisition, and few took up the chall
of limited growth. Exceptionally, James Thompson, in an article in 197.
in the *Library Association record* on stock revision argued that the probl
in British academic libraries was not yet acute. (6) It may be that the
majority of university librarians, not recognising themselves as deluded
emulators of Bodley's librarian, or their libraries as ever-increasing failure
yet felt that the combination of major universities, outstanding research
and large libraries might be more than coincidental. On the whole the
libraries which were engaged in relegating stock to reserve stores were
doing so because they had run out of space, and not because they believe
in the merits of slimming. As Brian Enright pointed out, that was the
situation in his own library at Newcastle until 'it seemed not inappropria
to dignify what had been recognised as a predicament and to use it as a
base for research', and to inaugurate a relegation project with British Library Research and Development financial support.

While university libraries were running out of accommodation, the UC
was running out of funds to provide further accommodation. The post-
Robbins expansion of universities had involved large-scale building programmes, especially for new universities which had to be created from
scratch. The chairman of the UGC, Sir Frederick Dainton, began his for
word to the Atkinson Report as follows: 'By the end of 1974 the University Grants Committee had come to the conclusion that they were
clearly not going to have enough resources, either in the short term or
the long term, to build new libraries at all universities on the scale neede
to match an indefinitely growing number of books. Even if this had bee
possible it was doubtful whether it would have been the most sensible
course to follow.' Accordingly the Working Party on Libraries was set u
in early 1975, consisting of three professors, one vice-chancellor, and
three librarians—two from universities (Brian Enright and Ogilvie Macke
and one nominated by the British Library (Maurice Line).

In directing the working party to consider minimum essential capital
requirements for university libraries, excluding copyright libraries, the
UGC referred specifically to the need to consider 'possible ways of prov
ing for the remote storage of books and periodicals in repositories to
avoid the necessity for a continual expansion of central library facilities

The first matter about which it asked for recommendations was 'the nature, scale and cost of the arrangements, including arrangements for closed access and remote storage, necessary to enable a university library to maintain an adequate open access library service and to place material in reserve at a rate broadly equivalent to the rate of accessions, with minimum damage to the service provided . . .' It also asked for broad guide-lines to assess, among other things, 'the amount of book storage required by a given library in its main buildings to meet essential requirements, on the assumption that suitable arrangements can be made for discarding material at a rate equivalent to the rate of accessions . . .' At first sight this appears to be asking for a steady-state library and to contradict the previous reference to placing *in reserve* at a rate broadly equivalent to the rate of accessions. However a closer reading suggests that in the particular context, the word 'discarding' either meant relegating to reserve and remote storage alone, or included some disposal, but did not imply disposing of one volume for every volume acquired. This is not an insignificant point since the interpretation of the actual recommendations of the report, the criticism levelled at it and the defence raised on its behalf, all involve the question of the degree of disposal entailed.

The formula which emerged when the working party's report was first made available in April 1976, was based on the concept of the 'self-renewing library, that is, a library of limited size in which beyond a certain point material should be reduced at a rate related to the rate of acquisition' (page 16). The report was first made available in duplicated form to vice-chancellors, to the press, and to certain organisations at a press conference in April 1976. The definition of the concept quoted here is taken, however, from the printed version published in July that year, whereas the original duplicated version referred to a rate 'approaching' the rate of acquisition. This amendment was circulated by the UGC because it was thought to clarify the concept.

Even in its amended form the principle was strongly criticised, particularly in academic institutions, some even coining the phrase the 'self-destroying library'. We may well ask what's in a name, but there was a general feeling that in its attempt to find a satisfactory description (perhaps to avoid any reference to 'steady-state', a phrase in disrepute among many librarians, and never very popular among astronomers) it had come up with something which smacked of the public relations consultant. The implication of self-improvement is not subtle enough; to cry 'New lamps for old' is to invite suspicion.

But serious criticism of the concept was based on the feeling that one cannot improve a research library by what amounts to a long-term replacement of its stock. Clearly new and up-to-date material must be acquired and out-dated editions must be removed from open shelves and may be discarded. But the argument ran that 'little-used' does not necessarily mean obsolete, and a single use by a scholar, leading to important discoveries, may justify the retention of a volume scarcely used previously. SCONUL stated, in a document agreed at its autumn 1976 conference, and later submitted to the UGC, 'It is the conviction of those librarians (concerned to make adequate provision of material for the support of worth-while research within their universities) that the ability to range freely among large collections of academically sound bookstocks is one of the most valuable assets of the university scholar.'

Criticism of the Atkinson Report thus took as its main target the principle of self-renewal. The question to what extent discard would be related to acquisition and thus how nearly would 'steady-state' be approached was left open in the Atkinson Report. But if the principle were adopted in the long term, it would appear that libraries which had all the open access accommodation to which the new norms entitled them and had filled reserve stores with the equivalent of five years' accessions, would be compelled to discard one volume for every volume acquired. At least, it would receive no UGC grant to provide further accommodation and this looks very much like zero-growth. However since the UGC has adopted the Atkinson proposals on a provisional basis and intends to review its policy in the light of experience over the ensuing two or three years, few libraries will have reached capacity by then, and the question may remain unanswered.

It is probably appropriate for the purposes of this chapter to discuss Atkinson as a proposal for strictly limited size university libraries, 'in which new acquisitions will be offset to a considerable extent by withdrawals', as the chairman of the UGC says in his foreword. Not zero, but low growth.

The main basis for this proposal is clearly the shortage of capital fund available to the UGC. One measure it could have adopted would have been to make no allocations for library building for five or ten years, to announce the fact to universities, and to leave them to take whatever steps they could to retain a library service. It is interesting to speculate what would have happened—after, that is, the screams had died away. Presumably, those universities with empty buildings would convert them into bookstores, those with reserve funds would seek out and purchase

40

disused factories and schools (measures which had already been adopted by a number of universities before Atkinson), some might have raised loans to build stores or new libraries, others might have persuaded philanthropists to perpetuate their names in steel and concrete. Many would have found material to sell or give away, and most would have taken a hard look at their acquisition levels.

The UGC no doubt felt that it would have failed to discharge its obligation to universities if it left a university entirely to its own devices with regard to its library, which the Atkinson Report from the start considers of great importance, emphasising the point by assigning it a capital letter for the first and only time: 'The Library is the core of a university. As a resource, it occupies the central and primary place, because it serves all the functions of a university—teaching and research, the creation of new knowledge and the transmission to posterity of the learning and culture of the present and the past.' The 1921 annual report of the UGC made a similar point in an oft-quoted paragraph. (7)

It sought therefore to find a means of ensuring the maintenance of university library services without the funds to expand main libraries. At this point it is as well to be reminded that the UGC does not take direct responsibility for library services. Its role is to provide for recurrent needs within a block grant to universities, leaving the library allocation to them individually, and to provide for the needs of expansion by capital grants for buildings based on space norms which it revises from time to time, taking into account the prevailing financial position. Any allocation it could consider making in a period of severe financial stringency would involve the laying down of norms which identified those libraries with the greatest need, at a time when virtually no funds were available anyway.

It was this consideration which prompted the Atkinson Committee to put forward suggestions as to how a university library might use available space, and to provide the UGC with a basis for making future allocations. In arriving at these proposals the working party worked through certain considerations; what was a reasonable minimum provision of shelving for the self-renewing library of a given size, what provision should be made for future growth, what benefits might be derived from the use of compact storage, microforms, further interlending, local cooperation, what was involved in selecting material for withdrawal, the characteristics of different forms of reserve storage, the scale of storage and the requirements of reader places. On the basis of an examination of the statistics collected from universities of the meterage of occupied shelving against student numbers, it proposed that 3.8 metres of shelving per student

41

should be adequate for normal working purposes, assuming some use of microforms and reliance on interlending and local cooperation; and local reserve storage sufficient to house the equivalent of five years' acquisition

The use of reserve storage is outlined in an important paragraph in the report (no 29):

> We have suggested that it is feasible and economic to withdraw annually from the main open access stock a proportion of a library's stock which is a considerable fraction of its annual acquisitions ten years previously. A significant proportion of every library's stock is little used and heavy use tends to be concentrated on a relatively small proportion of the total stock. The difficulty is that of deciding what to withdraw. Replies to our questionnaires indicated that in about fifteen out of forty-six libraries no reduction of the existing stock was undertaken, and in other cases this work clearly has a relatively low priority. This is probably due to the high cost of the process of selection and the actual withdrawal operation, and partly to reluctanc to withdraw material which originally cost a great deal of money to acquire, catalogue, and perhaps bind. Selection for withdrawal can be done either by category, or by individual judgement applied to each item. The former method is rough and ready but relatively chea the latter is academically preferable but may well require many hours of work by highly qualified staff.

There are a number of points made in this paragraph which are basic to a discussion on the limited size library. Certainly the reference to a 'considerable fraction of its annual acquisitions ten years previously' doe not represent steady-state unless acquisitions begin to fall a very great deal over a decade. What it does suggest on the other hand is continual growth, a possibility which is not promised by the proposed norms whic impose a ceiling on accommodation and therefore on expansion. It is clear that the report intends to leave vague the level of withdrawal, and this makes evaluation of the principle difficult. Equally vague is the stat ment that a significant proportion of stock is little used, understandably so since there is no accurate information available. Everyone would agre that there are books on the open shelves of some libraries which could b relegated without loss. This is an uncontroversial statement; whether the number is large or small may depend on one's viewpoint.

But everyone would agree with the statement that 'the difficulty is that of deciding what to withdraw', if, that is, it is to be a 'significant proportion'. The paragraph concedes one of the difficulties inherent in the relegation procedure. The reference to the questionnaire sent to

42

libraries attributing the low priority given to stock reduction 'partly to reluctance to withdraw material which originally cost a great deal of money to acquire, catalogue, and perhaps bind', is an interesting point, but it is arguable how many librarians are concerned about the original price of books in stock or their value in terms of past labour. Few librarians would hesitate to discard obsolete shelving or furniture. Rather than to identify a weakness for hoarding, it would be better to recognise a tendency to leave alone until space runs out, and a reluctance to accept the argument that the library would be improved if little-used material were removed. The opinion 'its presence on the open shelves may still be useful' is at least arguable. The opinion 'we paid too much for it then to throw it away now' is not tenable.

This chapter is concerned with arguments in the UK on whatever approximates to the steady-state library, and not with a detailed examination of the Atkinson Report iself. However this document, as now accepted by the UGC, a body which is the official grant-giving organisation in the UK for universities and their libraries, may be said to be the first official declaration, backed by the means to apply it in financial terms, of the nearest practical approximation to zero-growth. It must to that extent be unique in the world. It may be said that the university libraries of Great Britain are officially, and for the time being, self-renewing libraries. As far as can be judged, if the concept were applied over a number of years, then many would become steady-state libraries. Reaction therefore to the report is crucial to a consideration of the acceptability of the concept.

What is probably the first publicly expressed opinion appeared as the main editorial of the *Times higher educational supplement* for April 30 1976 (8), less than a week after the launching of the report at a press conference. This leader suggested that while we should expect a public branch library to 'self-renew', to freshen its stock and remove little-used material, 'surely the strength of a university library is not to be assessed merely by the intensity of use of its stock, but must include as an outstanding element its ability to support research and it is in this respect that so-called "little-used stock", conveniently available plays an important part in the research potential of the university'. It further went on to state that 'the books that academics recommend and librarians select are by and large for permanent retention, and librarians and academics have worked together over the years to strengthen their libraries in this way.' On the question of collection-building, it was forthright: 'While university libraries cannot and should not hope to be comprehensive, they must be capable

43

of supporting research; staff and research students do not want to spend all their vacations in London, Oxford and Cambridge, and their terms waiting for books on inter-library loan.'

SCONUL issued a preliminary statement after a special meeting held early in the summer following the report's publication. Its main criticism were that recommendations affecting the long-term management of library were made on the limited basis of financial and economic constraints, that there was insufficient evidence to support such far-reaching recommendations, that the growth referred to by the working party arose out of the implementation of the Robbins Report on university expansion, and the measures which the UGC had adopted would attempt to deal wit the symptoms rather than the causes, since libraries are an expression of the patterns of teaching and research of the institutions which they serve SCONUL considered that self-renewal was a crude instrument for dealing with a complex problem, that it was based upon inadequate research, that it paid too little regard to the needs of scholarship especially in the humanities, and that even in economic terms the report had established no adequate argument for self-renewal.

This preliminary statement was followed in October by a fuller document agreed by the conference and forwarded to the UGC. In his reply the chairman defended the report and made a number of points, which in his capacity as President of the Library Association for 1977, he has reiterated in addresses to librarians around the country.

The main arguments in favour of the adoption of the report centre around the critical financial situation the UGC found itself in at the end of 1974. There was a pressing need to devise a fair method for distributi the meagre funds available so that hardship would be shared, if not mitigated, so that library services could be preserved. The norms which had been adopted for assessing comparative needs were intended not as crude instruments but as guides to be applied with judgement and discretion to the consideration of claims for accommodation by individual university libraries; and the measure had been taken on an interim basis and were subject to review after two or three years, during which time attem would be made to assess their effects and to seek further information on which to base future planning. Arising out of the decisions of the report the UGC set up a Steering Group on Library Research early in 1977, to study what problems required further investigation, and to act accordingly, in consultation with research organisations and other interested bodies. The point that the UGC is anxious to emphasise is that while it has adopted measures which are unpopular, it is keeping

an open mind on the whole matter and is open to constructive suggestions.

There can be no dissension from the view that the measures are unpopular. The protests from SCONUL were followed by a document from
the Association of University Teachers. (9) In its opening section, writing
of the self-renewing library, its statement was uncompromising:

The concept is wrong from the very start. Existing university libraries
have not reached optimum size or composition. They need to grow
at a far greater rate than the UGC would allow to support the quite
genuine needs of both teaching and research, and they cannot, without
serious damage to both teaching and research, reduce their holdings
of older materials at the pace the UGC would apparently require.
Learning and knowledge are not finite and cannot be founded on artificially constricted libraries. It would be more accurate for the UGC
to talk of 'slow death' than of self-renewal.

Individual academics and librarians also joined the attack in the correspondence columns, principally of the *Times higher educational supplement*, which also in its issue of December 31 1976 carried an article
examining the attitudes of some university librarians based on interviews. (10)
There were a few letters counter-attacking the views of university librarians,
notably from a small number of polytechnic librarians. The grounds of
these criticisms were substantially the elements of the arguments for the
steady-state library; that is, that university librarians should emerge from
the collector's syndrome and recognise that service depends on the efficient
exploitation of an active up-to-date stock stripped of the dross of past
acquisitions.

In a detailed appraisal of the Atkinson Report by A J Loveday, published in the *Journal of librarianship* in January 1977, the important point
was made that the terms of reference given to the working party did not
include 'any suggestion that there should be a full-scale review of the
philosophy upon which university library provision had in the past been
based, and which hitherto had received the whole-hearted support of the
UGC.' (11) In other words, it might be said, the UGC had asked for relegation policies and got self-renewal. It did not get the costings which it
asked for and it did not get any indication of the optimum size of a library
(which it did not ask for but which is required for an appreciation of self-
renewal).

The Committee of Vice-Chancellors and Principals issued a document
in May 1977, based on the responses of individual universities. It accepted
the critical position regarding capital provision, it welcomed the UGC's

decision to undertake further studies into the implications of the new policy (the formation of the steering group) and whilst agreeing with many of the comments made by individual institutions it chose not to reiterate them but to indicate on their basis what aspects of the proposals most required further research. Since 'any reduction in library provision . . . necessarily has repercussions on academic activities, any consideration of a new policy must start with indentification of the nature of the services required to support adequately the teaching and research activities of the various faculties . . .'. It questioned the validity of basing book capacity on a student number basis. It accepted that simple norms applied sensitively were preferable to 'an exhaustive set of inflexible criteria', but it would have welcomed some indication of what special circumstances would be taken into account in assessing individual claims for accommodation. It accepted the need for reserve stores and indeed emphasised that relegation was not a new activity in university libraries, but it considered that 'it remains to be demonstrated that substantial savings of space can be achieved by the application of the self-renewing principle without damaging a library's quality.'

Noting the widespread view that the implications of the Atkinson recommendations simply involve a transfer from capital to recurrent expenditure with no genuine savings, the CVCP indicated that information was needed on the costs involved especially in the 'labour-intensive operation of selecting books for withdrawal', as well as on the costs of providing local reserve storage to obviate large-scale disposal. It was particularly concerned to establish what the position of the British Library was in relation to the Atkinson recommendation that material discarded from libraries might be offered to the British Library Lending Division. Could the BLLD absorb it, coult it handle the additional lending load, what would be the additional cost to public funds, and to individual borrowing libraries, and what would be their influence over pricing and acquisitions policies of the British Library? As a contribution to the discussions the CVCP proposed further investigations into the use of closed access, of loan-financed library accommodation and of local and regional collaboration.

This document is one of the latest major contributions to the discussion a discussion which the Atkinson Report may be said to have stimulated. Indeed, it has been said that if for nothing else, it could for that reason be called a success. Paradoxically, one result has been to create total agreement on one point; that further information and study are needed before any long-term policy can be established for university libraries.

Even if elements on both sides hope and expect that further information will support their argument, the truth can do nothing but good; if, that is, the truth can be established. What it is hoped may emerge is a reduction of ignorance.

However, a number of questions pose themselves. Can we arrive at the minimum size, or the optimum size, or even the maximum size of library to support the work of individual universities? What are the financial implications of various policies of library management? Can we measure the effectiveness of libraries with any accuracy and, if so, how would the measures be applied in a period of economic constraint? To hope for accurate answers to these and all the other questions that the debate throws up is too much to expect. University librarians will remain in the future in their present predicament of 'decision-making in an uncertain environment', only hoping for less uncertainty.

The latest contributions to the discussion, published by the Library Management Research Unit, are the proceedings of a seminar among some two dozen invited participants under the title *The future of library collections*. (12) It is not a collection of the arguments on both sides of the self-renewing line, though it includes many of them in its discussions. It is primarily a consideration in detail of the way forward from our present position, emphasising the need to add to the stock of knowledge, and to plan ahead, as, it is hoped, influential members of our own autonomous institutions, and as cooperating librarians, concerned with the quality of national resources.

The critical shortage of capital for building and the subsequent Atkinson Report have brought about a radical change. Whether individual libraries pursue previous policies, or change course, librarians will be working in a different environment with a sharpened awareness of the issues involved.

REFERENCES

1 University Grants Committee *Capital provision for university libraries; report of a working party* London, HMSO, 1976.

2 University Grants Committee *Report of the Committee on Libraries* (the Parry Report) London, HMSO, 1967.

3 *The art of the librarian; a collection of original papers from the library of the University of Newcastle upon Tyne* Oriel Press, 1973, 1-13.

4 D J Urquhart 'The library user and his needs. Research into library services in higher education' Papers presented at a conference held at the University of London on Friday November 3 1967. London, Society for Research into Higher Education, 1968, 1-5.

5 Keith Barr and Maurice Line (eds) *Essays on information and libraries: Festschrift for Donald Urquhart* London, Bingley; Hamden, Conn, Linnet, 1975.

6 J Thompson 'Revision of stock in academic libraries' *Library Association record* 75 (3), March 1973, 41-44.

7 University Grants Committee *Report of the University Grants Committee* February 3 1921. Cmd 1163. London, HMSO, 1921.

8 'First aid for libraries' *Times higher educational supplement* April 30 1976, no 236, 16.

9 Association of University Teachers 'University libraries' *AUT bulletin* November issue 1976, no 65, 11-12.

10 Frances Gibb 'Universities will fight to shelve Atkinson plan for libraries' *Times higher educational supplement* December 31, 1976, no 27 5.

11 Anthony J Loveday 'An appraisal of the Report of the University Grants Committee Working Party on Capital Provision for University Libraries (the Atkinson Report)' *Journal of librarianship* 9 (1), 1977, 17-28.

12 J W Blackwood (ed) *The future of library collections; proceedings of a seminar held by the Library Management Research Unit, University of Technology, Loughborough, 21-23 March 1977* Loughborough, 1977. (L M R U report no 7.)

THE STATE OF THE ARGUMENT: AUSTRALIA

John Horacek

REACTIONS to any document are chiefly affected by two factors—its intrinsic content, and the context within which it is read. The latter, of course, can be entirely different from the context within which it is written. Thus the following account of the Australian reaction (or, indeed, lack of reaction) to the proposals of the Atkinson Committee will need to establish the context—the present state of collection development in Australian academic libraries and the relationship of this to total national resources. And this in turn has to be seen as part of the national growth of Australia. Accordingly, the first part of this chapter will take the form of an overview of the present situation, and its immediate origins.

In 1946, Australia had a population of seven and a half million. There were six universities, one in each state, teaching a total of 25,585 students. If one compares the number of undergraduates to the eligible population (ie the seventeen to twenty-two years age group) one finds that 3.5 per cent were being taught at the universities. Thirty years later, the total population has topped fourteen million; there were eighteen universities catering and competing for 153,465 students who represent 9.5 per cent of the same age group. In short, the growth has been considerable in both absolute and relative terms.

The great boom period was during the 1960s, and followed on from the publication of the *Report of the Committee of Inquiry into the Future of Australian Universities* (Chairman, Sir Keith Murray) and the creation of the Australian Universities Commission (AUC).

Alongside the universities there are the colleges of advanced education, dubbed equal but different, which still have a technological basis, though the courses offered have diversified greatly over the years. The main difference between the universities and the colleges at present is that the latter support very little research, and do not offer higher degrees by course work. The colleges achieved 'respectability' after the publication of the *Report of the Committee on the Future of Tertiary Education in Australia* in

49

1964-65 (Chairman, Sir Leslie Martin). They have been supervised by the Commission on Advanced Education, previously the Commonwealth Advisory Committee on Advanced Education.

The Commission on Advanced Education took under its wing in 1973 the former teachers' colleges, which had previously been administered by the education departments of the states. This change increased the number of institutions with which it was concerned from thirty-nine to seventy-eight.

This should explain why it is not possible to give enrolment statistics for this second group of institutions (the teachers' colleges and the colleges of advanced education) which would be directly comparable to those for the universities. The figures are also not comparable because the enrolments include a far greater proportion of part-time students. Nevertheless the growth in student numbers is as striking as that for universities—in 1965 total enrolments (not including the teachers' colleges) were 24,330; in 1976 the estimated numbers were 134,580, this time including enrolments in the teachers' colleges.

By way of a last word, it should be stated that the two bodies mentioned above (the Australian Universities Commission and the Commission on Advanced Education), along with the Technical and Further Education Commission (concerned with post-secondary, non-degree courses) have been renamed 'Councils' and enfolded into a Tertiary Education Commission. There is also now under way a long term investigation by a Committee of Inquiry into Education and Training, which is to 'review possible developments up to 2000' in all areas of post-secondary learning.

The number of institutions has increased, the number of users has increased, and we would expect the bibliographic resources of the libraries of the institutions also to be increasing. Unquestionably there has been growth, and in a recent article, Harrison Bryan, Librarian of Sydney University, noted that figures relating the student population to the collection size reveal that 'Australian students would seem to be no longer greatly disadvantaged compared with their British colleagues.' (1) However, to this optimistic statement he adds two caveats, one referring to the 'enormous supplementary resources easily available to the British university librarian and to the British student'; the other concerned with the lack of material for advanced study and research in Australian university libraries.

It has been the second of these points which has been often stressed in many of the official pronouncements on university libraries in Australia Thus the *Fifth report* (1972) of the Australian Universities Commission includes (paragraph 11.20) the following statement: 'The commission recognises that all Australian university libraries face severe difficulties in building up and maintaining good scholarly collections, and that Australian scholars in the humanities in comparison with colleagues in other countries suffer severely from lack of materials for original work'. Note is also taken of the problems which occur in the humanities and social sciences when new interests evolve (whether as a result of the establishment of new disciplines or the personal research activities of new staff members), which existing library resources cannot serve. 'Many universities take into account the needs for equipment when introducing new activities or appointing new members in scientific disciplines; universities might also employ a similar approach with respect to library material in the humanities and social sciences'. And since, within the recurrent funds assigned to universities, there is a special category of funds for equipment, it was only a short step for the commission to take to recommend (12.10) 'a substantial equipment grant which is intended to provide for the various equipment requirements of the university, including the filling of gaps in library material and the purchase of computing equipment'. Such funds in the commission's view should be used not for the purchase of single monographs or current periodicals but for 'multi-volume works of reference or back runs of journals and the purchase of collections of books which are related in the sense that they deal with a certain area of study'.

Unfortunately this radical step did not benefit libraries quite as much as the commission had intended. Its *Sixth report* (1975) includes statistics which show that, of the money available for equipment (excluding computers), 8.5 per cent was allocated to libraries. 'This was slightly lower than the commission had anticipated'. (12.17) It should also be noted that the allocations which individual universities made to their libraries ranged from 16.9 per cent to 0.9 per cent.

However, Bryan's basic point stands—considerable gains were made in the provision of bibliographical resources. The Munn-Pitt survey of 1933 showed that the existing six university libraries held something over half a million volumes. In 1973, just forty years later, the bookstock of eighteen universities had grown to over eight million volumes of monographs and bound serials, not to mention microform and audiovisual material.

But collection growth generally implies larger buildings; and the *Sixth report*, under the caption 'Future development of library services', makes this cautionary, and prophetic, statement: 'At the present average growth rate of library collections of 10 per cent per annum, library stocks will double in size every seven years. The need for stack accommodation will thus continue to grow steadily. Since the growth rate of student numbers is likely to be falling, the funding of library extensions may prove difficult (12.22) Nevertheless, the commission did recommend several extensions to libraries for the 1976-78 triennium, but these fell victim to the almost total cut on capital expenditure subsequently imposed.

It is also worth noting that the Universities Commission *Report for 1977-79* (the altered dates for the triennium being due to a Labour govern ment decision to have 1976 as a non-triennial year) in several places speaks of a no-growth situation, with university enrolments kept to 1976 levels. Just as the student population is static, so university budgets are being kept to a minimum rate of growth. The major casualty of this policy has been the building programme: no major works were initiated in 1977 and many projects which had been recommended in the *Sixth report* will not be undertaken within this triennium. The *Sixth report* had recommended some half dozen library buildings, but only two are scheduled for 1978, and none for 1979.

As far as the colleges of advanced education are concerned, the biblio-graphical situation is different. It is an understatement to say that their libraries are modest in size compared to those of the universities—although their educational status was raised, up-grading of their facilities to an equivalent level was not as easy to achieve. The Commission on Advanced Education has signified its concern quite strongly in its reports, and several special grants were made, to assist the libraries in their endeavours to make up lost ground. There were two grants of half a million dollars, in 1966 and 1969, and a third (and final) grant of five million in 1972. Despite this support, there is no doubt that not enough progress has been made—al colleges are under considerable pressure to diversify their teaching pro-grammes, and the effects of this on library resources and budgets are seldoi adequately considered, despite the token attention that course accreditatio bodies pay to examining library resources in the areas in question.

Thus the colleges are catering for a larger student body and a wider curriculum. This to a large extent cancels out the fact that the actual sums devoted to materials for college libraries have increased quite signifi-cantly.

The cut-backs referred to above, and the stress on a no-growth situation have been continued into 1978, according to the guidelines on education spending announced in June 1977. According to these guidelines, univer-sities will receive the same amount as in 1977, and colleges less than 1 per cent more. Furthermore, there is now no allowance for inflation in any area except salaries—previously, universities and colleges received supple-mentary funds to compensate for the effects of inflation on buildings programmes, library acquisitions, etc. In other words, the 'same' means 'less'.

The effects of the government's determined attempts to control inflation by limiting spending on the public sector, including education, will only become apparent as time passes; that Australian education has had its fat years is certain, but it is doubtful how well it can survive the lean ones. And if the lean years continue, a climate similar to that which created the Atkinson Report could develop.

Australian interest in the Atkinson Report and its recommendations followed a perhaps predictable pattern. The first news of the report was gleaned either via contacts in Britain, or via airmail editions of the *Times* and the *Times higher education supplement*, and prompted a lot of urgent orders for copies of the report by airmail. The copies duly arrived, and were read and digested, though by this time there was a growing accretion of secondary material.

The reactions to the report crystallised in two main ways—articles and papers, of which there have to date been four, and a series of CAUL letters. CAUL is the Committee of Australian University Librarians, a body which is held together rather loosely, in between its annual meetings, by a round-robin style correspondence. Such correspondence is therefore not private though not actually published, and is a valuable reflection of attitudes towards issues and problems affecting university librarianship in Australia.

The CAUL correspondence has been trickling through the system, the first letter having been written in December 1976. So far, about two thirds of the university librarians have commented on the matter, and certain trends can be observed. Firstly, the suggestion has been made and generally accepted that a small committee of three librarians should prepare a document which would set out the implications of the Atkinson concept for Australian university libraries, spelling out the differences between the situation in the UK and that in Australia. The committee's membership represents the range of Australian libraries—the large, the small, and the new.

However, in tandem with the idea of taking some action there runs a contrary belief which is based on the fact that few Australian vice-chancellors have expressed much interest in the Atkinson Report to date, and that therefore it would be more politic to leave things as they are. This view is not in conflict with the idea of a document being prepared, it merely suggests that any such report should be regarded as insurance, and only made available when needed or asked for. This school of thought also points to the fact that discussion in the UK is still proceeding vigorously, and that the Universities Grants Commission is still, so to speak, hedging its bets about the implementation of the report.

The correspondence has also drawn attention to the point that, Atkinson or no Atkinson, the current economic climate in Australia is not conducive to large-scale building programmes, and that therefore the report and its recommendations are not relevant. Another matter, raised in passing by one respondent, is that some Australian university libraries are well below any standards of self-sufficiency, even Atkinsonian ones, and that these need not feel as threatened as the others.

This correspondence, as I have said, reflects attitudes; specific points however are hardly touched on. In fact, the correspondence was based on two papers, an unpublished report by Elizabeth Watson of the Australian National University, entitled 'The concept of the "steady-state" library' (a paper which subsequently developed into the essay in this book), and a paper by Harrison Bryan entitled 'The perpetuation of inadequacy' in *Australian academic and research libraries*. A third paper, by Colin R Taylor (then Divisional Librarian for Readers' Services at the University of Western Australia and now Chief Librarian of the South Australian Institute of Technology) has recently been published in *Vestes* (the journal of the Federation of Australian University Staff Associations). (2) The fourth paper on the Atkinson Report to be disseminated in Australia is again by Harrison Bryan, this time more imaginatively entitled 'A cloud no bigger than a man's hand'. This paper was not published but delivered in March 1977 as an address to the Victorian Division of the University and College Library Section of the Library Association of Australia.

There appears to have been no reference to, or comment on, the Atkinson Report in the *Australian library journal*.

Of the articles mentioned above, the first three follow basically the same pattern as the first, providing an exposition of the ideas contained in the report along with critical comments on its methodology and assumptions, before proceeding to examine its implications in the Australian context, and its transplantability. Harrison Bryan's second paper is able to assume a basic acquaintance with the ideas in the report, and so contains less exposition, stressing instead both the general theory of self-renewal and its applicability to Australia.

I propose to give here only a brief outline of the general points made in these papers; more space will be devoted to the specific problems of applying the Atkinson guidelines in Australia.

Elizabeth Watson comments in her unpublished paper and her chapter in this book on the interesting phenomenon that what is fundamentally a reaction to a set of historical and, more importantly, economic data, has been transformed into a new philosophy for libraries. The Alexandrian, comprehensive library is being contrasted with the self-renewing phoenix library which is not only supposedly less expensive but easier to use. Watson notes that on two points the proponents and the critics of 'steady-state' libraries agree—the need for less expensive storage for less used material, and the desirability of carrying out 'collection-review', which would include weeding. But she lists many more points of disagreement, including: the difficulty of identifying a 'mature' collection; the lack of criteria for weeding, beyond use statistics; the decreased browsing value of lean libraries; the lack of proof that a large collection is harder to use; the lack of guidelines for maintaining integrity of collections in different subject areas; the lack of proof that a 'steady-state' library will save much money in the long term; the lack of definition of the pressures on space in a library, beyond a growing collection; the difficulty of actually weeding a collection which aims to cater for research as well as undergraduate needs. Watson points to the great dearth of information on the use of libraries and the needs of students and researchers, especially in the humanities and in interdisciplinary studies.

Bryan's *AARL* paper focuses upon criticism of two crucial points. (3) One is that in his view the Atkinson Committee set up an Aunt Sally in implying that university librarians were guilty of a 'thoughtless acceptance of indefinite growth'. The other is that the working party first asked 'whether it was reasonable to relate the size of the library required directly to the number of students', and then, having calculated an average of shelving per student over a range of British university libraries, proceeded to use this as a measure without any further justification or discussion of the 'reasonability'. To Bryan, stress on student numbers can only be justified in the area of undergraduate studies, and the dominant factor affecting the required size of a collection is the spread of teaching in the parent institution. In his view, every library must attain a 'minimal viable degree of self-sufficiency', on the lines of the Clapp-Jordan formula. After quoting some of the British reactions, he states that 'A conclusion which it is very difficult to reject is that the Atkinson Report is an extremely dangerous document, presenting as it does the apparently reasonable exposition of an extremely glib over-simplification'. (4)

Taylor takes a much less gloomy view. He considers 'the norms reasonable and the suggestions for the slowing down of ever-increasing size in university libraries to be sensible as well as an economic necessity', though he would like to see some weighting in favour of the smaller universities, to enable them to build bookstocks larger than their enrolment figures would allow. His conclusion is that 'there doesn't seem to be a case for an alarmist reaction . . . amongst Australian universities, because the repor certainly does not advocate the no-growth "self-renewing" library so freely described by the press'.

Obviously there is a divergence of views here. It might be slightly cynical to suggest as a partial explanation the fact that the Australian National University and the University of Sydney exceed their Atkinsonia entitlements whilst the University of Western Australia is slightly below, and could enjoy unchecked growth for some five years more!

This leads to the consideration of the effects produced by translating Atkinson into 'Strine' (Australian). Watson only touches on this, but raises one of the vital issues by commenting on the lack of collections in Australia which would be comparable in extent to the British Library Reference Division and the libraries of the Universities of Oxford and Cambridge.

Bryan's *AARL* article includes a table which relates book-stock to student numbers for all Australian university libraries for 1975. This indicates that six of the eighteen have reached the limit allowed, though one of these is the newly established Griffith University (1975), which is hence a special case. Of the remaining five, Bryan suggests that two (Tasmania with 325,819 volumes and Flinders with 337,616) would not 'be pleased to be halted . . . at a point well short of serious research potential'. The formula for reader places produces figures 'so far above the British norm as to cast at least some doubt on its usefulness'.

Bryan next comments on the 'profoundly different library environment in Australia', partly explicable by what the Australian historian Geoffrey Blainey has referred to as the 'tyranny of distance'–in this case both the distance of Australia from the great book collections of Europe and America and the distance between libraries on the Australian continent itself. The absence of any library comparable to the British Library or the Library of Congress and the lack of a 'central library of last resort' like the Lending Division of the British Library make the Atkinsonian proposals in his view 'doubly impracticable for Australian conditions'.

Like Bryan, Taylor has tabulated the Atkinsonian projections for Australian university libraries–his results are different, due to a differing formula for translating part-time students to educational full-timers but not significantly so. The higher proportion of seating places in Australia puzzles him–'Perhaps someone else would like to explain why the Australian university student needs more seating space in his university library than his British counterpart, because no really obvious reasons spring to my mind'.

Bryan's 'A cloud no bigger than a man's hand' develops some of the points made in his earlier article. Having outlined what he calls a 'minimum tolerable size' for a library, below which it is non-viable, and having firmly anchored this size not to student numbers but to the breadth of the teaching and research programme of the institution in conjunction with the different publication rates for the various disciplines, Bryan then calmly states that, for the University of Sydney, 'three to four million volumes in immediate access is not too constricting'! In his view, 'as a whole, academic libraries in Australia are so far from their appropriate minimum levels of sufficiency that, while it seems both logical and sensible to accept the inevitability of a policy of self-renewal, the application of that policy should be far from imminent'.

In the Australian context the Atkinsonian formula is seen as being inadequate, even apart from the basic fallacy of the nexus with student numbers, since 'a main characteristic of the Australian university, vis a vis its British counterpart, is the breadth of its teaching and, inevitably, the spread of its encouragement to research, thus driving its library increasingly into the fields of collecting where the requirement is singularly unrelated to student numbers'.

Again taking the Atkinsonian formula and projecting into the future (assuming stable student populations and accessions at 1975 rates), Bryan deduces that over the next ten years almost all the universities will have reached their point of stabilisation. He draws attention to the fact that at the James Cook University of North Queensland, at Townsville, 'a library with no major support within nearly a thousand miles, offering the PhD over a wide range of faculties, would be stabilised, or perhaps rather stagnated, at a total stock of 131,482 volumes. This looks like the classic reductio ad absurdum'.

He emphasises further that 'the minimal level of self-sufficiency for Australian academic libraries must be higher than for British libraries because of the triple problem of isolation that Australian libraries face: isolation from one another; lack of big city library back-up; isolation from great research collections'.

After these points Bryan moves on from considering the applicability of the Atkinson Report to Australia to the likelihood of its being applied. He sees the report as a possible threat, a cloud on the 'cloudless skies that characterise the present and future of academic library development in Australia'. He refers to the diminishing funds for academic institutions

57

and infers that funding authorities would therefore have some interest in Atkinson. 'Even before the appearance of the report there was some evidence of a specific AUC interest in library rationalisation with some unde tones of collection stabilisation'. Nevertheless, his forecast is a fairly favourable one since the present generation of vice-chancellors is attuned to library growth and has shown overall a very proper concern to preserve and advance the position of the library in the university. Still, the cloud is seen as a timely warning to librarians 'not to assume obdurate stances but to accept the inevitablity of a degree of limitation to . . . future operations'. Referring to the CAUL correspondence on the issue, he thinks that 'it would be wise to prepare . . . a statement'.

I am aware of only one other formalised Australian comment on the Atkinson report. This occurs in a detailed study conducted on behalf of the Commission on Advanced Education by Eric Wainwright and John Dean. (5) This study was published in October 1976 and represents a detailed and closely argued analysis of the various factors which affect the ability of a college library to meet the demands placed on it. From among statements made there which have a bearing on Atkinsonian proposals and methodology one could quote: 'There is strong evidence to suggest that the range of courses offered by an institution is a major, or even *the* major, factor in determining the requirements of a college library collection'. (6) 'Substantial extra library collection provision . . . may be required where a college does have a programme of the research-oriented type'. (7) 'Extra provision may need to be considered for college libraries situated in country areas'. (8) The report provides specific formulas for estimating the desirable size of a collection—the formulas take into accou the number of courses at various levels (two-year, three-year, post-gradua as well as the numbers of teaching staff and students. Similarly the required annual growth of a collection is seen as tied to exactly the same factors.

The report also finds that existing collections are inadequate when measured against such standards—sometimes quite tragically so. When dealing specifically with the 'no-growth' proposals, the authors state that:

In the CAE context, at least in the medium term, such a concept seems of dubious validity. Although a few of the metropolitan colleges may well reach their terminal size during the next one or two triennia, it seems unlikely that even at that stage changes in the composition of the college membership will not continue to occur. Variations in the proportion of part-time or external students may be expected to continue, while development of courses to meet changes in community demands or advances in knowledge may be expected to occur, and desirably so, into the indefinite future. Thus, whilst it may well be true that once colleges have reached, at least approximately, a stable state, the *rate* of growth of collections may decline, this may be seen merely as an extension of present trends. These appear to portend a slowing down of the development of new courses in CAE's. Hence we may expect a corresponding slackening in the rate of growth of their library collections, since much of the rapid recent increase in the size of college collections has been in order to provide a service for new course areas. In a 'steady-state' situation, collection increases arise largely as a result of the need to acquire new publications, both monograph and serial, which advance knowledge in the subject fields of interest to the college. We have assumed that in practice a wholly 'steady-state' situation is not likely to arise in Colleges of Advanced Education in the medium-term. (9)

However Bryan, in his meteorological survey of Australian post-secondary education refers to blue skies with 'an element of tattle-tale grey' for the universities; for colleges of advanced education 'the atmospheric conditions . . . are, on balance, still rather duller today'; and for the technical and further education sector 'future prospects are definitely on the smoggy side'.

Obviously the likelihood of steady-state style thinking spreading in Australia cannot be dismissed easily. I have referred to the fact that the funding bodies are already basing many decisions on the 'no-growth' concept. The guidelines issued by the Minister for Education are based on the expectation that the university sector will maintain its intake of students at the present level, and the same is true for the colleges.

Since the funding is being kept at the past year's level, there is therefore an almost inevitable backward movement for libraries, which will be purchasing fewer items unless the inflation affecting books levels off. Now this is not as critical as it would have been ten years ago; nevertheless, as the reports quoted earlier have stated quite definitely, there is still a want of depth in the collections of universities. Interlibrary loan figures provide an interesting barometer for estimating the pressures on collections in the libraries, and they indicate that the pressures are not lessening. Quite the contrary, as the following table of interlibrary borrowing shows:

| 1961 | 10 universities borrowed | 16,129 items |
| 1966 | 14 universities borrowed | 41,734 items |

| 1971 | 15 universities borrowed | 71,646 items |
| 1975 | 18 universities borrowed | 83,778 items |

Nor are all these requests satisfied locally; every reference librarian is quite used to receiving the following report from the National Library: 'No location in Australia', and therefore having to go overseas—it is estimated that over ten thousand items were sought overseas last year. No doubt no country can hope to satisfy all local needs, but it is obvious that Australia is still very short of the resources necessary to support the full range of research and teaching activity. Furthermore, the fact that the numbers of interlibrary borrowing have been rising in spite of increasing library resources suggests that there is a growing need which the reduced purchasing powers of the university libraries will only aggravate.

Nor has the National Library of Australia the collection which can answer these needs. Although it has grown rapidly, it is still (with its 1,625,000 volumes in mid-1976) smaller than the University of Sydney, and therefore not a library of last resort. Furthermore, its budget will not enable it to grow as its council and senior staff would wish it—imaginative ventures such as the project of buying comprehensively all the dissertations covered by the University Microfilms programme have been terminated due to financial constraints.

The statement of receipts and payments of the 1975/76 *Annual report* indicates that the National Library spent 1,870,286 dollars on what could be collectively termed materials. Given the responsibilities of the National Library this is quite inadequate, and contrasts badly with the nearly fourteen million dollars spent by universities.

It must be recognised that (except for some special collections held at the National Library and the state libraries, and some smaller, unique collections) the bibliographic resources of the university libraries represent the nearest Australian equivalent to the enormous accumulations of research materials represented by the British Library or the Library of Congress. Consequently any changes which affect university library developments affect the nation.

It is clear that those most disadvantaged by limits on library growth will be the scholars working in the areas of social sciences and humanities. The undergraduate is relatively well off—the libraries cater generously for his needs by providing multiple copies of prescribed reading, and by giving him a greater chance of finding a seat than he would expect to find in a British university.

The scientific researcher is not too badly off, since his needs are only partly bibliographical—laboratory and equipment provision in Australia being by all accounts adequate, certainly by British standards. The scientist also has the advantage of being able to draw upon the resources of a wide range of special libraries, especially those which form part of the chain of research institutes incorporated within the Commonwealth Scientific and Industrial Research Organisation. Many of these have strong holdings of serials and report literature, and also operate automated information retrieval services. Furthermore, in the final analysis, the scientist is interested largely in the latest research, and therefore the comparative newness of antipodean collections is not a problem—or so we are informed by those who have attempted comparative use studies for various disciplines.

But the historian, the political scientist, the economist, and the anthropologist are the ones whose needs are least well met—to take at random some of the disciplines from the broad range of humanities and social sciences. What is happening is that the collections they are working with already lack the depth of early publications, and, given budgetary restrictions, will in future lack comprehensiveness of new writing and research.

The various factors which brought about the Atkinsonian recommendations are starting to manifest themselves in Australia—growing pressures on storage space in libraries and reduced funding for tertiary education, especially in the area of capital expenditure. The Australian phenomenon of static student numbers (even though to an extent artificially induced) further reinforces these. There is therefore every possibility that the solutions suggested by the Atkinson Committee may be seriously considered as a suitable resolution. Yet the Australian context is radically different from the British one, and it is impossible (in my view) not to agree with Bryan when he states that whatever problems Atkinson creates for British university libraries, they would be twice as bad for the Australian university and college libraries. The fact that the majority of collections are below the proposed standards, in terms of the size of the collections, should not be taken as any guarantee—firstly, sooner or later it will put a brake on the growth of what are Australia's main libraries, and secondly, there is nothing sacred about the figure of 3.7 metres of books per full-time student. It could be increased or decreased as government funds for education expand or contract.

But one can also take the Atkinson Report positively, as a sign of the times and consequently as a stimulus to thought and planning for remedial action. Given the reality of reduced funding, what possible alternatives can be postulated to reduce the resulting disadvantages? One initiative of obvious importance is the National Library's BIBDATA project, which is

designed to be an on-line cataloguing service for a network of Australia's
major libraries. Whilst this is primarily a cataloguing system, with parall
overseas (most notably the British Library's MERLIN), it will have the
valuable side-effect of creating an on-line data base/union catalogue whic
will make the much-discussed but seldom-tried schemes for rationalisatic
of collecting more possible. It will also affect the speed with which inte
library loans can be transacted, a vital factor given the absence of any
equivalent to the British Library Lending Division. There is therefore a
need to press for the development of such a network to take the place o
the local self-sufficient libraries. The regional networks planned for Vic
(CAVAL—Cooperative Action by Victorian Academic Libraries) and Ne
South Wales (CLANN—College Libraries Activity Network in N S W)
whilst obviously more limited in their scope and power would also have
a role to play.

Another, equally obvious, avenue to be explored is the use of cooperative storage for less used materials. At present this question has be
receiving some thought, especially in the Sydney area, where the three
largest universities already operate their own out-of-library stores.

The survey here presented of the 'state of the argument' about steady
state libraries shows that during 1977 there had not been much thinking
or comment, at least in public, in Australia. Numerous issues have been
touched on, but none explored. But Bryan is surely right when he sees
that the Atkinson Report is a timely warning, which needs a positive response—which has to date not been forthcoming.

Australian university and college libraries are entering on a period wh
can be said to be less favourable than the preceding years have been. Th
restrictions affecting them are the general economic ones which can be
expected when a country is trying to break out of the grip of inflation.
To have these restrictions reinforced and codified into a philosophy base
on dubious assumptions (as Atkinson does) would be a serious handicap
for Australian libraries, especially since regulations tend to outlive the
circumstances that begot them, and the concept of 'no-growth' libraries
may persist into a time of flourishing economy.

In view of the national importance of Australian university libraries, i
is to be hoped that there will be wider debate of their present and future
requirements and that other groups, especially those representing users,
will take part in these discussions. The content of the Atkinson Report
may make it attractive to governmental bodies, but the context of the
Australian bibliographic scene should make it at least unattractive to
librarians and to the library users.

REFERENCES

1 Harrison Bryan 'Growth patterns of British and Australian University Libraries' *Australian academic and research libraries* 7(2), 1976, 102.

2 Colin R Taylor 'Capital provision for university libraries in the United Kingdom' *Vestes* 20(3), 1977, 40-43.

3 Harrison Bryan 'The perpetuation of inadequacy' *Australian academic and research libraries* 7(4), 1976, 213-221.

4 Ibid, 220.

5 E J Wainwright and J E Dean *Measures of adequacy for library collections in Australian colleges of advanced education* Perth, Western Australian Institute of Technology, 1976.

6 Ibid, vol I, 10.

7 Ibid, 12.

8 Ibid, 16.

9 Ibid, vol II, 12-13.

STEADY-STATE AND LIBRARY MANAGEMENT

Peter Durey

AT PRESENT there is a tendency to talk about 'steady-state' and 'zero-growth' as if these were new concepts in library management. Perhaps they are for some fortunate institutions but there are many librarians who can remember other periods of recession which had similar effects to those being caused by the current economic difficulties. Even the concept of the self-renewing library which has caused such a flurry of excitement in university circles in Great Britain is not really new. Maintaining a collection at a fixed size involves the use of procedures which have been followed by many public libraries for a very long time and which have also been applied to some areas of university library collections—notably those designed for undergraduate use. There ought then to be some accumulated managerial experience to assist the practitioner in these circumstances. If there is, very little of it seems to have found its way into print.

The major implication of steady-state for the library manager is that his or her job is likely to become a great deal more difficult. There will be a considerable increase in the amount of negotiation and argument in which the librarian is involved. It is obviously very much easier to say 'yes' to the majority of demands made on the library than it is to have to start evaluating competing demands and say 'no' to some of them. Although librarians are usually reluctant to admit that they have adequate financial resources there have been periods in the recent past when libraries in many developed western countries were comparatively affluent. As a result some library staff have, to some extent, lost the art of saying 'no'.

It has been my experience that interest in library finance is in inverse ratio to the adequacy of funds available. It is when funds are short and decisions have to be taken which have a direct bearing on the interests of the library users that there is increasing interest in the way in which these funds are allocated. In these circumstances the director of libraries may find that the methods used in the past to allocate resources are challenged for the first time. This may come as a shock to those who have known

64

little else but the growth pattern of the sixties and early seventies. Librarians in general have been accustomed to thinking in terms of expansion, of solving problems by asking for more money to pay for more staff and more library materials.

Until comparatively recently very little attention was paid to results to see whether value for money was actually being received. Cost-benefit analysis is a concept unfamiliar to the majority of librarians. It is also a technique which can be difficult to apply to library services. As Ruth Risebrow says (1) 'We can calculate the cost of storing materials as opposed to joining a network and borrowing them, but what is the cost of delay to the user? How do we cost or weight that? We know what the cost is of keeping a library open twenty-four hours a day, or twelve hours a day. What is the cost of closing it the other twelve hours? Is the cost the same for a future Einstein as it is for an ordinary graduate student or under-graduate or a faculty member? How do we evaluate our service?' My answer, not that it is much help, is that there are a great many of our activities which we as librarians cannot evaluate. Our clients have to do that for us and we have to hope that they will, perhaps with encouragement from us, be sufficiently vocal to complain in influential quarters when service falls below a level they consider acceptable. However, whether we like it or not, the cost-benefit approach is increasingly likely to be required in a no-growth situation and there are areas of library work where it can be readily applied—circulation and processing departments are obvious examples.

No-growth does not mean no-choice. The library director faced with a static budget, or even worse, one which is decreasing, does have some alternatives. The basic choice is an adjustment of the ratio of spending on staff, library materials, other expenditure. He can also consider the possibility of direct charges for some services. Most librarians contemplate this with reluctance but some libraries already charge for inter-library loans and charges for searches of computerised data bases are relatively common.

It is undoubtedly true, as Martin suggests (2), that no general theory of library budgeting exists for a no-increase situation but in his examination of some sample budgetary histories he tries to illustrate the problem of balancing expenditure on staff with that on books and periodicals and he makes it clear that with a decreasing budget neither books or other expenditure can absorb the whole cut without severe dislocations or even failure to meet basic library goals. A major portion of any reduction must therefore come from expenditure on personnel.

65

Before any decision can be made on adjustment to the budget the director needs to accumulate as much information as possible to make sure that whatever is done will have the least harmful effect possible on library services. This is of course provided the director feels that the fun allocated to the library represent a fair decision by the funding authority in terms of that authority's total resources. If it is felt that this is not so and that the library is being unfairly treated then the director may choos to publicise the retrenchment. This can be done for instance by cutting staff in public areas so that there is an obvious effect in the shortening o opening hours or by the withdrawal of heavily used services. This is a pl which has to be used with caution. There is still a need for the director to have undertaken a full review of staffing. It is all very well trying to enlist public support by drawing attention to the financial plight of the library by an obvious cut back in services. The library director will soon lose credibility however, if it can be shown that the required saving coul have been achieved by other staff economies which would not have dire affected the public.

How does the library director set about deciding whether staffing leve are appropriate throughout the library system? It would be very conven if there was a body of standards which laid down appropriate staffing fo the discharge of the various tasks performed by libraries. Unfortunately those 'standards' which do exist may provide some guidance for general assessment of the staffing level of the library but they do not provide m help in determining appropriate levels of staffing for various library ope ations. Indeed, given the wide variation among libraries in the way in which even basic operations are performed it is difficult to see how they could do so. The library director is, therefore, faced with evaluating the work of every member of staff in the system to try to discover whether the existing structure provides for the most efficient operation possible of every aspect of the work of the library. Stated baldly like this it can be said with confidence that there is no library system where the results will show that a state of perfection has been achieved.

The frightening aspect of a survey of this kind is that it can mean tha particular jobs have to be described in a great amount of detail and som person (or persons) has to spend a great deal of time in its compilation. Thus at a time when the library may already have begun to feel the pinc the director may be faced with a very difficult decision; whether to add an extra burden to staff who are already finding that they cannot cope with the existing workload. It may be a counsel of perfection but a wi administrator will have made studies of this kind as part of normal management procedures even before financial problems compel an evaluation of staffing levels.

What is actually done will usually have to be a compromise based on the staff resources available. Some help in deciding on the design of a staffing survey can be obtained from a literature search. However the library director will soon find that since there is a total lack of accepted definitions for the vocabulary of librarianship (for example, what does 'original cataloguing' mean?) that while he may be able to obtain some guidance in the techniques of measuring the time taken to perform various library tasks he will run across a great many problems in his attempts to compare the results with performance elsewhere. Nevertheless, an exercise of this kind can produce results. Masterson in a paper (3) on the use of work study in Newcastle-upon-Tyne Polytechnic library (which has for some years based its staffing on the results of work studies) comments 'It is virtually impossible to make meaningful comparisons with other surveys without an intimate knowledge of the systems surveyed . . . [However] from the data we have been able to plan staffing for various work-loads and to adjust work distribution with differing staff numbers. We have also been able to pinpoint work done by grades of staff and so deploy them in the face of staff shortages.'

Those North American libraries which have taken part in the Management Review and Analysis Program ought to be in a peculiarly favourable position to make the kind of adjustment necessary in a steady-state library. MRAP was developed by the Office of University Library Management Studies of the Association of Research Libraries as an assisted self-study approach to improving the management of large university and research libraries. Over twenty libraries have applied MRAP so far. As might be expected, there seem to be some variations in the practical results reported by participants, although there appears to be fairly general agreement that application of MRAP results in improved management practices. A more recent offshoot has been the Academic Library Development Program intended for small and medium sized academic libraries. If the aims outlined for the project can be realised than it has many attractions for the administrator of a steady-state library. Morein describes the aims of ALDP as follows (4):

1 Provide a means for libraries to improve their performance through more effective use of their human and material resources.

2 Furnish processes, procedures, worksheets, and guidelines which a library can follow in evaluating its services, operations, and management practices.

3 Create within the library a more positive, 'proactive' attitude toward change.

4 Increase the library's problem-solving capabilities.

5 Expand the staff's knowledge, skills, and abilities through an experiential 'learning-by-doing' approach.

6 Furnish a model process which will enable academic libraries to develop more systematic, analytical work methods.

7 Develop the interpersonal skills of the staff so that individuals can work more effectively in group situations.

When MRAP was first developed it was stated that the aim was to ma the basic manual and program generally available after testing in selected libraries. Unfortunately, despite extensive testing it still does not appear that the program has reached the stage when it can be made generally available. Most of the reports issued so far seem to have found involvement of staff from the Office of University Library Management Studies essential to the success of the local project. MRAP has been criticised fc the very heavy expenditure of staff time involved and also for its inheren inward-looking nature. Nevertheless it would seem to provide a splendid opportunity to collect the detailed information on mission and performa which the manager of a steady-state library will need before he begins re distributing resources.

Expenditure on books and periodicals

In the past librarians have usually tended to look on that part of the budget devoted to the purchase of books and periodicals as sacrosanct. The first recourse in times of economic difficulty has been to make cuts in staffing and in other areas of expenditure. Now there are indications that this attitude is changing and that librarians are prepared to give equ scrutiny to expenditure on library materials.

Some fundamental assumptions in collection development policies ar being questioned. The most notable candidate for reassessment is 'Big is Beautiful'. Librarians have always been reluctant to admit to the pursui of numbers as a desirable aim in collection building. It is patently obvio that quality is as important as size of collection. Unfortunately in pract size has too often been taken as a synonym for quality and used as the only yardstick (as, for example, in the criteria for membership of the Association of Research Libraries in North America). Now it is being increasingly admitted that not only size and quality but *use* is a facto which must be taken into account when assessing the value of a particular collection.

Academic librarians have, in the past tended to be extremely defensive about questions on the use of the collections they administer. They have some right on their side in their claims that they are building a resource for the future as well as for current use. All of us have reason to be grateful to those of our predecessors who collected material which has increased in value and use, and to curse those who missed the opportunity to obtain material which we now require. But we have to be careful that this is not an excuse for unselective buying of material which is unlikely to justify its purchase either now or in the future. There is little doubt that during the sixties and early seventies there was a great deal of buying of this kind, particularly in affluent North America. Some of the blanket-order purchasing schemes for instance produced collections of material which it is difficult to see will ever be required. and a number of institutions have purchased comprehensive and expensive collections of microtext which are little-used. In my view it is entirely proper that library administrators should initiate procedures to review current usage of library material to see whether resources seem to be being extended in the most useful manner. This is particularly important in small and medium sized institutions but not irrelevant to the needs of large institutions. The kind of procedures developed will depend on the staff resources available and while an in-depth survey of particular areas by subject specialist may be desirable a simple subject sample surveyed for usage within a given period may produce some interesting results. The nightmarish escalation in periodical costs can make local usage an important factor in considering whether a subscription should be retained and those without any system of recording current use of serials should consider whether they need to introduce one.

When considering projects for resource sharing librarians have frequently made the point that the contents of the university library reflect what is taught and studied at that university. For each subject a minimum amount of material is required irrespective of how few students or research workers are involved. The difficulty lies in defining 'minimum' but it would seem that too often the distinction between what was really needed at a local as compared with a regional or national level has been ignored. The current economic climate means that resources cannot be assessed solely in local terms and the library administrator will have to consider resource sharing far more frequently than he has done in the past. Librarians have also argued that it is not possible to 'rationalise' library collections unless academic institutions 'rationalise' teaching and research. In the past, university autonomy (and jealousy!) has tended to discourage the development of agreements in specialisation among institutions. Economic stringency should assist this type of negotiation and librarians ought to be among those pushing for agreements of this kind to be reached where possible to avoid unnecessary duplication of library materials.

At the 1976 Pittsburgh conference on resource sharing in libraries Professor Leon Montgomery remarked that 'one of the interesting paradoxes in resource sharing is: with sufficient funds, library administrators don't need resource sharing. With insufficient funds, library administrators can't afford resource sharing.' (5) I find myself in complete disagreement with both of these statements. The real problems for the library administrator are deciding whether a cooperative programme will provide a satisfactory service at local level and forecasting the effect on costs.

Talk about resource sharing assumes that there are resources to share. It is obvious that libraries in countries with a strong national library, many large collections and a well developed inter-library loan service are in a far better situation to cope with the effect of restrictions on their own purchases than those in areas which have neither good central resources nor efficient means of sharing what they have. Libraries in Europe and in North America are fortunate in the number of alternative sources of supply which are at their disposal. Libraries in Africa, Asia, Latin America or Australasia are generally not so fortunate. As far as Australasia is concerned, Australian resources have grown out of all recognition in the recent past and in New Zealand, although the changes have not been quite so dramatic, there has been a transformation at least in the university library scene. However, New Zealand is a country with a small number of libraries and with a National Library facing enormous financial and accommodation problems. Miraculously an efficient inter-library loan service does operate and access to local resources is reasonable. But these local resources are so thinly spread that, for example, the abandonment of a serial subscription by one library can have a significant impact on national as well as local resources. The smaller and more isolated the country the greater the problems—if New Zealand thinks it has problems what about those of the University of the South Pacific in Fiji?

One of the most worrying factors about the current situation is that no one knows how long the economic difficulties are going to last or indeed whether the situation will deteriorate still further. This in itself provides a number of problems for the director of libraries whose decisions would not be the same if he knew that, for example, budgetary restrictions are likely to last for one year instead of five. So far, many institutions have made only the kind of review of their purchases which prudent financial management should in any case have compelled. But the longer economic difficulties continue the more danger there is that cuts will have to be made not in items of little use but in resources usually considered indispensable. This is most likely to become a serious problem when expenditure on periodicals has to be reduced. Deciding priorities can be extraordinarily difficult for the librarian faced with the necessity for cutting back journal subscriptions when the subscription list has already been reduced to those considered highly useful. All the librarian can do is to arm himself or herself with as much information as possible about usage and local and national resources before coming to a decision.

One major problem of budgeting in a steady-state library is apportioning the expenditure between books and periodicals. There is, of course, no magic proportion which will be suitable for all situations but while there has been escalation in the costs of all library materials the costs of many periodicals have reached frightening heights. If expenditure on this area of the budget is unrestrained the librarian can easily find himself in the position of having no funds at all for monographs. The library administrator, therefore, needs to project periodicals expenditure into the future, to assess the effect and to take measures accordingly. The publishers of many periodicals appear to have conspired to make things as difficult as possible for the librarian even to estimate accurately the current cost of periodical subscriptions. Librarians really must begin to question far more vigorously than they have done in the past a system which allows retrospective price increases, unannounced additional volumes, enormous price increases without explanation. Economic difficulties compel us to try to achieve some much needed reforms in journal publishing.

Since most librarians have, at some stage in their career, been faced with the need to obtain missing volumes of a periodical cancelled in some earlier financial crisis, the decision to cancel a periodical is usually undertaken very reluctantly. In the recent past many libraries have had to face substantial reductions in their periodical holdings and the stories of how they did it are beginning to appear in the professional press (for example, in the pages of the new journal originally and inelegantly called *The de-acquisitions librarian* and now rechristened *Collection management*). Decisions have to be taken in terms of the financial resources available and bearing in mind other local, regional and national holdings as well as local use. The process is not likely to be an easy one and a great deal of staff time will have to be expended if the result is to be satisfactory. Much of this time will be spent in canvassing the opinions of faculty in an area which is of major concern to them.

71

Staff

One of the major problems which steady-state can cause library mana
is the effect that it has on the staff of the library. For many people,
association with an institution which is experiencing zero-growth is
psychologically unsettling. There are, after all, a number of not unreaso
able fears. There may be uncertainty about job security and also about
the ability to continue to perform the job satisfactorily in changed circu
stances. It is not only the library director who faces problems when bud
restrictions force a change in the services previously offered by the librar
Those directly involved in the service may in fact receive the bulk of
complaints and resent this if they feel that the library administrators are
not exerting themselves to explain the reasons why the situation has
arisen.

Communication, always a problem, becomes even more important in
the steady-state library. It is essential that all members of the library sta
are as fully informed as possible about the financial position of the libra
and that they are involved in any decisions which affect the service given
by the library. Participatory management has become an increasingly in
portant issue but there are wide divergences of opinion as to its suitabilit
for application to libraries. While one can find examples of systems whi
appear to have tied themselves up in an almost irretrievably complicated
network of interlocking committees, I believe that there is a far better
chance of a system weathering the problems of steady-state with the wel
informed staff which a system of participatory management should produce.

For an individual staff member it may be extremely difficult to see
the lines of authority in the library structure, to realise where he or she
fits into the overall pattern and to feel that when a problem arises there
is a system which allows for individual involvement in the decision making process. This is of course the kind of situation for which the Manage
ment Review and Analysis Program was developed. While the program
has undoubtedly involved a large number of librarians in thinking about
the problems facing the library they serve it has critics. Dr William Axfc
comments (6):

> Because it specifically limits itself to a study of internal relationships
> and procedures, there are serious questions regarding the MRAP's
> potential for producing the attitudinal structural changes necessary
> to make academic libraries more effective in resource utilisation, and
> through this, more responsive to user needs during a prolonged budge
> crisis. In some respects the MRAP reflects the fact that in spite of the

72

blossoming romance between academic library administrators and modern management theory and techniques, it has not yet produced the all consuming passion for constantly monitoring performance which will guarantee their effectiveness. Lacking this catalyst, the romance has not really matured into the productive marriage it was anticipated to be.

Steady-state is a misnomer for the situation as it applies to library staff for it usually affects job content and conditions. A major problem for the library director is how to prepare his staff and then how best to implement the changes. Advocates of participatory management claim that it makes staff more flexible and responsive to change and I am inclined to agree even though I know that there are examples of institutions where the reverse seems to have happened. Of course we must remember that 'participatory management' is not an abstract concept—people are involved. The person with a circumscribed view of his or her own responsibilities is not necessarily going to change through having been involved in some group discussions.

One result of zero-growth may be the need to re-deploy library staff. If the library intake of books and periodicals is reduced then it seems logical to expect that there will come a point at which the staff in the departments ordering, cataloguing and processing material should be reduced. The director may have a problem in deciding the precise moment when the staff should be reduced since it is a rare head of department who will suggest this. However, since these departments have an end-product in terms of books ordered, catalogued etc, it is easier than in some other areas of library operations to calculate output per staff member in the past and to base discussion on staff reductions on this figure calculated against the current drop in workload. 'Catching up on the backlog' may temporarily avert the evil day when the administrator has to make a decision but it cannot be deferred indefinitely if the library remains in a difficult economic situation. Eventually a decision to reduce staff may have to be taken and it may be extremely difficult to maintain a proper balance of professional and clerical staff. If a high proportion of the professional staff have tenure then it may be necessary to dismiss so many support staff that librarians find themselves heavily involved in non-professional duties.

If the staff are being relocated rather than being dismissed this will usually mean a move from technical services to public services. Now this, in fact, is an attractive proposition to many library administrators who are keen to reduce the number of library staff working behind the scenes

73

in favour of an increase in the number of those working directly with th
users of the library. There can be problems in achieving this. In the ma
jority of libraries senior staff will have been recruited to a particular pos
ition and the qualities which have fitted a person for a post in technical
services may not be suitable for public services. There may be a problem
too if a staff member feels that he does not wish to make a move. He/sh
may do so if faced with a dismissal as an alternative but a move undertaken in this spirit is not likely to be oversuccessful. The library directo
has therefore to give very careful thought to proposed relocations and t
try to ensure as far as possible that moves of this kind can be shown to
be appropriate for the person concerned. Almost inevitably some form
of retraining will be necessary. For most institutions this will mean in-
service training and this can involve an additional load on supervisory
staff. The supervisory staff must therefore be fully involved in the plan
of any programmes of this kind and must be made aware of the econom
reasons which have made the programme necessary.

The administrator has to face the problem that there will almost certainly be some members of staff who will not be suitable for relocation
or for whom alternative work cannot be found. It will be his or her pain
ful duty to terminate their employment. I have expressed elsewhere my
views on the dismissal of staff in these circumstances (7):

When staff have to be dismissed because of a cutback in finance it is
particularly important that the criteria for termination should be
scrupulously fair. The maxim 'last in first out' is not a bad one to
follow, although it is not free from causing anomalies. The temptatic
to use the occasion to get rid of library staff who have been trouble-
some to the library administration is of course a strong one, but dis-
missing employees who have, for example, been active in union affai
is asking for trouble unless the dismissal can be clearly shown to be
unrelated to these activities. The library administration must always
be very careful to make sure that the reasons for terminating particul
employees will stand against a charge of victimisation.'

Where there are union agreements governing the conditions of service
or all or part of the library staff then these may be expected to include
some clauses covering redundancy and the administrator will then of co
have to follow the procedures which have been agreed.

In fact in a unionised library the administrator can expect to have an
increased amount of negotiation with unions in a period of zero-growth
This may occur not only when there are what union agreements tend to
refer to as 'layoffs' but also when the library wishes not to replace staff

who resign. Librarians with little experience of union agreements may find it difficult to visualise constraints of this kind but it is not unusual for agreements to include a clause requiring the posting of vacancies within a certain time limit and for the employer to justify his action to the union if for any reason this is not done. In these circumstances, therefore, the employer cannot unilaterally decide to freeze positions if staff members resign or retire or if a person granted maternity leave decides not to return. The action the employer wishes to take can only be taken by agreement with the union.

Future recruitment policies may well be affected if a library moves into a position of zero-growth. In this situation a great deal depends on the adaptability of staff and the library may hesitate to recruit personnel whose qualifications are too specialised. This is where the generalist comes into his or her own. While in the past it has been common for junior un-qualified library staff to be appointed to the system rather than to a particular post it has been relatively unusual for more senior appointments to be made in this way. In future it may be necessary to contemplate making all appointments, except the most senior ones, to a grade rather than a post in order to maintain as much flexibility as possible. This, of course, goes completely counter to the tendency in academic libraries in recent years to recruit an increasing number of subject specialists. It is less likely to happen in the United States where library administrators face a tangled web of employment regulations which may preclude them from making appointments to a system rather than a specific post. Even there, however, the right is usually retained to downgrade a post when it becomes vacant and this is likely to become more common as library directors try to save money by altering the ratio of professional to para-professional staff. If there is not also a redistribution of duties there is likely to be staff unrest.

Steady-state is likely to bring with it some changes in emphasis in the work of library staff. One area where there is likely to be a significant difference is a substantial increase in monitoring the collections so that future selection can be based more accurately on patterns of usage. Very few academic libraries have done much work of this kind in the past and the recent work on stock control in university libraries has been concerned largely with predicting areas of heavy demand and adjusting the systems to satisfy this.

The heavily criticised Atkinson Report (8) focused attention in Britain on the idea of a 'self-renewing library'. Although academic librarians are familiar with the idea of cooperative storage of less used items and there are some successful schemes of this kind which have been in operation for many years, the idea that the majority of university libraries should be balancing their new acquisitions by withdrawal of older stock came as a considerable shock. While I believe the case was over-simplified and the results can be shown to be demonstrably absurd in particular instances there seems little doubt that university librarians have been too prone to consider that once material has been acquired, catalogued and shelved then the librarian's duty has been discharged until someone cannot find the book he or she wants.

Librarians now have to accept that uncontrolled growth is impossible and to devise monitoring systems accordingly. If the Atkinson recommendations were to be followed, some British institutions have calculated that they would need very heavy expenditure on staff to be able to carry out the considerable amount of stock relegation which it recommends. However, ignoring the extremes of the report, most large academic libraries are going to be faced with the need for much more stock editing than in the past and library directors will need to plan the appropriate strategies and take into account their implications in terms of library staffing.

One area of expenditure where directors are likely to have to weigh their decisions far more carefully than they have previously done is automation and its effect on staffing. The wheel has come full circle. In the early days of the application of the computer to library problems, staff savings figured largely in the sales talk. The experience of many libraries having shown that staff saving was not automatic, the emphasis has shifted to the additional tasks which could be performed. Now in the current economic situation the emphasis is changing back again to possible saving in staff. In the meantime experience seems to have shown that the development of a comprehensive local automation programme is so complex a task that only the very largest institutions have the resources to attempt it successfully. As a result many libraries are turning with relief to co-operative ventures. Is this in fact likely to produce the savings which are required? Richard de Gennaro sounds a note of caution (9):

Although these new approaches to library automation promise to be much more effective and produce greater savings, particularly in cataloguing and processing operations, these savings will be rapidly offset by inflation and diminishing budgets, and libraries will still be left with serious long-term fiscal problems. This is because these problems originate in over-ambitious acquisitions policies and are only exacerbated by costly traditional processing routines. Computer technology will have its greatest payoff for libraries as it is more widely used as a tool to assist librarians in developing and operating networks and other new mechanisms for sharing resources on a national and international scale.

It is of course worth noting that complicated technology may not necessarily provide the best solution to the problem. Computers have played a minor part in the rise of the most successful example of rapid access to a national resource, ie the British Lending Library at Boston Spa.

The director of a library in a zero-growth situation is likely to be attracted to involvement in a network if he feels that the result will be a saving in costs or that by participation he will be able to maintain service. But there can be some important implications for the library staff if the library begins to rely on external organisations for some aspects of work which were formerly under local control.

If it is known that a principal reason for entering into a network agreement is staff saving then there is likely to be a very considerable drop in morale if the limits of staff saving and the way in which these are to be achieved are not known in advance. The administrator is in a very difficult situation. He has to prove his judgement to the financial agency that subscription to this system will save x staff positions, he wants to let those staff he will be retaining know that their jobs are secure, he does not want to announce redundancies too early in case his calculations are wrong. If the administrator is prudent he will have received agreement that staff savings can be achieved either by relocation or by normal wastage. If this is not possible then the administrator should not go ahead with a decision to participate in a network until he is virtually certain that his judgement on staffing levels is correct. If it is obvious from the start that certain members of staff are going to be dismissed then the people in those posts are not going to wait until the system is viable before they start looking for another job.

Some of the other fears of staff involved in a change to a cooperative system are similar to those feared by those facing automation programmes: fears that the individual will not be able to cope, and fears that the network will not perform as well as the individual system it replaces. The first of these alas sometimes proves true, but in his preliminary planning the administrator should have assessed the capabilities of the personnel available and made rearrangements in staffing if necessary. There may be fears that there will be significant changes in the conditions of work. Not everyone wants to spend their day gazing at a visual display unit. There may also be a fear that the job may be dehumanised—that somehow by surrendering local autonomy the individual becomes a cog in a very large machine operating by remote control. The answer to many of these problems seems to lie in good communication and the opportunity to participate in the decisions which must be taken.

For the library director the decision to participate in a particular network may be extraordinarily difficult if participation is linked to a required reduction in staff. This is a condition which faced some clients of the Ohio College Library Center. They could not have found the decision easy because although this is a well reported system the pattern which emerges is confusing to say the least. Stecher has illustrated the inconsistencies in the published data which made any kind of assessment particularly difficult. (10) However, Hewitt says:

> The impact of the network on cataloguing staff levels is much less salient than its effect on turn round time. Sixty-three per cent of the charter member libraries had reduced cataloguing staff at the time of the survey (1974) with a total of 76.83 net positions dropped . . .
> The majority of libraries adequately staffed prior to use of the system should find it possible to decrease the size of cataloguing staff. Whether or not such decreases will be equivalent to payments to OCLC will depend for the most part on the aggressive pursuit of this objective by administrators in individual libraries. (11)

The last point shows the importance of motivation. If cost savings are a principal motive for involvement in a cooperative venture then it is fairly clear that a library director will be keen to see that cost savings are achieved to vindicate his own judgement.

Library costs other than staff, books and periodicals

These include building maintenance, cleaning, heating, lighting, postage, telephones, telex, equipment, stationery, printing, travel. Practice varies among institutions and all or none of these items may be assigned to the library budget. Cost increases in basic services supplied from outside the institution may cause very considerable problems for the library director particularly if he has to work within the limits of an inflexible budget. I remember the national library of one developing country which was unable to send any letters at the end of its financial year because its postage budget was exhausted! The energy crisis and the greatly increased cost of power has made many institutions scrutinise this area of expenditure very closely. Libraries cannot expect to escape this.

Some institutions have tried to encourage power saving by offering to allocate all or some of any resultant financial saving to the part of the institution concerned. This may seem attractive to a hard-pressed library director but it may also be exceedingly difficult to achieve any worthwhile results. Too often in the past building design has ignored future running costs. We cannot say we were not warned. As long ago as 1965 Keyes Metcalf in his monumental *Planning academic and research library buildings* (12) had some criticisms which have even greater relevance now than at the time they were made:

> Too often librarians and other administrative officers for that matter, have given little thought to lighting costs because these have not been included in the library budget but have been paid directly by the institution. The author recently talked with a librarian in a fine new library with attractive lighting, given unusually high intensity even for the present time—over 100 foot-candles—and asked what the lighting bill came to. The reply was 'We don't know yet, but it has been suggested that it would come to some 400 dollars a month'. A little figuring, carried out by multiplying the wattage used in each bay by the number of bays, the hours of opening a week, and the cost per kilowatt hour of current used, indicated that 4,000 dollars a month would be closer to the mark.

Library administrators now have to face the fact that expenditure on lighting and heating may not go unquestioned and they have to be prepared to consider economies by turning down thermostats, removing some fluorescent tubes, installing a switching system which automatically turns off lighting in areas when daylight reaches a certain intensity and so on. While being cooperative the administrator also has to try to make sure that economies do not reduce the level of provision below that which provides reasonable conditions for readers. It is worth remembering, as Keyes Metcalf pointed out, that there seems to be no evidence that, in earlier years when lower light intensities were customary, there was more defective vision than at present or that reading speed and comprehension were less than they are now. In addition European library patrons appear to thrive in buildings heated to temperatures much lower than those customary in many North American institutions.

Steady-state in terms of library accommodation means a period of make-do-and-mend for library administrators. A moratorium on building additional space still allows the librarian several possible courses of action as far as current library space is concerned. Probably the first step is to review the current arrangement of the collections. Not all areas of stock expand at the same rate and in most libraries there will be some areas where the original allocation of space to a particular subject was too

79

generous. Planning stock movement to make the best use of available space can be a complicated exercise. It is, unfortunately, one which librarians are likely to become all too familiar with in any period of economic crisis. It can involve a great deal of work for the library staff and there are likely to be problems with staff morale unless the end product can be seen to justify the amount of work involved—there comes a point when the administrator must call a halt to moving stock if the space gained is minimal. If there is the possibility of finance for extra shelving then the furnishing layout needs to be reconsidered. The librarian may be faced with a very difficult choice if, as in many buildings, the only way extra shelving can be inserted is by the sacrifice of reader space. However, some recent layouts do use space extravagantly and in leaner times can be re-designed for a much higher rate of book occupancy.

If the possibilities of moving round the stock and inserting extra shelving have been exhausted then removal of material to storage elsewhere is the next consideration. Storage accommodation inevitably costs money but it should cost much less than additional new accommodation on the library site and may therefore still be feasible in the current economic climate. In a few areas it may be possible to arrange cooperative storage ventures of the kind that already exist but my guess is that they will remain the exception rather than the rule. Once storage has been secured the librarian faces a very considerable problem in deciding what to put into it. The library which has a record in each book of the last time it was lent for home reading has a very important advantage in designing a relegation system.

If the library is completely full, if there is no possibility of additional shelving or storage, and no significant amount of little-used material which can be discarded, but material continues to arrive, then I think that no amount of ingenuity will provide a solution. I do not really see why the librarian should try to conceal the situation provided it is not of his or her making. Let the books pile up on the window sills and the floor. Perhaps if sufficient senior members of the university fall over them a solution will be found (and if the most influential senior members of the university do not use the library perhaps it would be useful to send them photographs of the chaos).

Conclusion

I hope that my comments have sustained my initial diagnosis that the implication of steady-state for the library administrator is that his or her job will become increasingly complicated. There will be a pressing need to accumulate considerable amounts of data about the functions of the library and the way in which these are performed. This data is required to assist the administrator in calculating complicated permutations of financial allocations to staff, books and periodicals and other areas of library expenditure to achieve the best possible result. In order to do this the librarian may find himself trying to use techniques of cost-benefit analysis which are not always particularly well suited to an exercise of this kind. There may also be a need to adjust patterns of recruitment and conditions of service in order to obtain library staff who are sufficiently flexible to adjust to the changing work patterns which steady-state can bring.

Practical examples of the way in which a number of librarians have tried to adjust to some of the problems of steady-state budgets are contained in the proceedings of the 'Managing under austerity' conference held at Stanford University in June 1976. (13) From these papers there emerges a picture of librarians scrutinising every item of expenditure to see where savings can be made and resources re-allocated. Many of the themes are familiar. Stretching the book dollar by bargaining for discounts, buying review copies of new books, buying paperbacks rather than hardbacks, cutting library opening hours, looking for cheaper alternatives to full binding, changing photocopying machines to get a better deal, converting professional positions to non-professional are some of the topics discussed.

Some of the innovations are reminiscent of the depression years of the thirties. California Institute of Technology, for example, has instituted a register of personal subscriptions to journals by faculty members which it is reported has enabled the cancellation of some duplicate or less-used items. One method of re-allocating resources is unlikely to be widely imitated. Caltech managed to fund its OCLC terminal from the insurance money it received for publications destroyed in a commercial bindery fire!

There have been some alarming indications in the recent past that management in some of the largest libraries was operating under very considerable strain. Economic crisis and zero-growth may turn out to be a blessing in disguise if it provides an opportunity for these institutions to reassess their objectives. For small and medium sized institutions however, the frustrations in management are likely to outweigh any possible benefits.

REFERENCES

1 Ruth Risebrow *Service or organization: two views—three responses* (Occasional papers 1) Tucson, University of Arizona Library, 1974, 16-19.

2 Murray Martin 'Budgeting strategies: coping with a changing fiscal environment' *Journal of academic librarianship* 2 (6), 1977, 297-302.

3 W A J Masterson 'Work study in a polytechnic library' *Aslib proceedings* 28 (9), September 1976, 288-304.

4 P Grady Morein and others 'The Academic Library Development Program' *College and research libraries* 38 (1), January 1977, 37-45.

5 Leon Montgomery from Pittsburgh conference on resource sharing in libraries in *Journal of academic librarianship* 2 (5), November 1976, 246-7.

6 M William Axford 'The interrelations of structure governance and effective resource utilization in academic libraries' *Library trends* 23 April 1975, 551-571.

7 Peter Durey *Staff management in university and college libraries* Oxford, Pergamon, 1976, 147.

8 University Grants Committee *Capital provision for university libraries; a report of a working party* London, HMSO, 1976.

9 Richard de Gennaro 'Austerity, technology and resource sharing: research libraries face the future' *Library journal* 100, 15 May 1975, 917-923.

10 G Stecher 'Shared cataloguing: an exercise in costing OCLC' *Australian academic and research libraries* 7 (1), March 1976, 1-11; see also the letter by Hogan in the December 1976 issue of the same journal, 263-4; and Stecher's response March 1977, 42-3.

11 Joe A Hewitt 'The impact of OCLC' *American libraries* 7 (5), May 1976, 268-275.

12 Keyes D Metcalf *Planning academic and research library buildings* New York, McGraw-Hill, 1965, 185-186.

13 John C Heyeck *Managing under austerity: a conference for privately supported academic libraries* Stanford, Stanford University, 1976.

GROWTH CONTROL
IN THE RESEARCH LIBRARY

John Dean

THE STEADY exponential growth in library collections as a result of external factors such as increases in knowledge and scholarly output, technological advances, increase in book and periodical production, has been discussed by a number of writers. (1) The possible effect librarians might (or should) have on some of these external factors, and the responsibility librarians have for encouraging growth in other ways, has also been discussed at length. (2) The accelerating growth in book production, the over-indulgence of collection-builders past, the prospects of shrinking space and evidence of growing user dissatisfaction, seem to have created a sense of frantic helplessness on the part of research librarians. 'One is left with a depressing suspicion', states B J Enright, 'that academic libraries are out of control, having little influence over the costs of their materials or their operation, the level of traffic or the pattern of growth . . . ' (3)

Enright likens the academic library to the cyclotron in quoting Lord Bowden's remarks that ' . . . the united efforts of all the staff are only sufficient to keep the machine on the verge of operation.' Enright and others have pointed out that unrestrained growth leading to oversized collections does not simply consist of logistical and financial problems of space and costs, but leads inevitably to inconvenience and intellectual problems for users as ' . . . library obesity creates a negative browsing situation and an unhelpful collection bias.' (4) The most visible result of growth is the problem of shrinking space, thus most of the strategies developed by libraries in response, have been concerned with seeking more space. According to a recent study by Claudia Schorrig most of the libraries responding to her survey would attempt to deal with lack of space in traditional fashion (by building a new library, 10.1 per cent; extending existing buildings, 44.9 per cent; utilising present space more efficiently by compact shelving, 28.1 per cent; developing a separate storage facility, 27 per cent; converting runs of periodicals to microfilm, 52.8 per cent). Only 24.7 per cent would seek other solutions. (5)

Clearly, most librarians still appear to be less concerned with the problems of size and growth than with the symptomatic problem of lack of space. This apparent failure to recognise that size can cause problems is perhaps understandable in a profession that has extolled size as a virtue for so long. That sheer size alone is not indicative of library effectiveness has been amply demonstrated by the literature. That the reverse may well be true, ie that increases in scale seem to increase the percentage of unused books and the unit costs of processing and servicing, has been noted by Buckland and Hindle who quote the British SCONUL study that '... the larger the one, the greater the other.' (6) If increases in collection sizes diminish effectiveness (in terms of ease of utilisation and browsability and unit costs), then it must logically follow that the traditional strategies developed to manage, indeed facilitate, increased size will create more ineffective collections. The stabilisation of size and reversal of growth would seem to be ways of answering the demands for more shelf space, and maintaining or enhancing library effectiveness. The point at which growth should be stabilised (optimum size) and the nature and 'quality' of a collection, are dependent upon the collection's purpose. This purpose should be defined by a careful examination of the goals and objectives of the library, and those of its parent institution.

Goals and objectives

Statements on the goals and objectives of academic libraries tend toward ambiguity, usually as a consequence of difficulties in identifying a clear statement of mission from the parent institution. In some cases the institutional goals, long- and short-range plans, and projections on resource allocation, have to be assembled piecemeal by the library from statements of the administration, press releases, annual reports, programme announcements, etc.

The kinds of information necessary to the formulation of institutional goals and objectives should include: projections on size and constitution of the student body (undergraduate to graduate ratio); the number and type of interdisciplinary and interdivisional programmes planned; future changes in faculty appointments; number and types of new programmes planned; number and types of old programmes to be discontinued; new directions in organisation, both administrative and academic; changes in relationships to other institutions; physical changes (new building construction, etc). Occasionally a statement to the library by the administration and/or faculty in one area (eg 'no more library building will be permitted'), will provide a focus for library goals and objectives in another

Often the process of formulation of institutional goals and objectives, and the strategies developed for the gaining of essential information, will suggest a mechanism for continuous review and evaluation. Such a mechanism must also be an integral part of library planning activity in the process of establishing objectives, determining courses of action, allocating resources and evaluating progress.

Library management planning functions in the establishment of these goals and objectives has been dealt with elsewhere, and the need for specificity in the statements of objectives clearly demonstrated. Policy statements regarding the development of the collection should be a logical extension of the goals and objectives statements of the institution and the library. Having established policies stating the collection development objectives of the library in support of the institutional requirements, some methods should be developed to enable the determination of how successfully the collection is meeting those requirements.

Collection evaluation

Several methods have been developed to evaluate the collection's success or failure in meeting the goals and objectives of the library. The methods range from highly quantitative to highly subjective, their effectiveness dependent upon factors such as the nature and availability of data, the size and nature of the collection, resources available, extent of faculty support. None of the methods is entirely free from some degree of subjectivity, and the results can often be interpreted in a variety of ways. One of the most complete and lucid surveys of the methods of evaluation is that produced by George S Bonn 'Evaluation of the collection'. (7) Bonn describes five basic methods: 1) compiling statistics on holdings, use, expenditures; 2) checking list, catalogues, bibliographies; 3) obtaining opinions from regular users; 4) examining the collection directly; 5) applying standards (using various of the foregoing methods).

1 *The compiling of statistics* Bonn identifies ten categories of things normally counted: gross size (volumes, catalogue entries, serial titles, etc); volumes added per year (total numbers, by subject, per capita, etc); formulae ('acceptable core plus volumes per student, per faculty, per undergraduate field, per graduate field'); comparisons (comparability between prior studies at same library, and/or other similar libraries); subject balance (proportional analysis by class, duplicates, authors, dates, courses offered, etc); unfilled requests (unavailability of books, serials, etc); inter-library loan requests; optimum size (determined by level of reader satisfaction); circulation (counts by type of readers, subjects, publication date, period

of heaviest use); expenditures (on books, serials, salaries, cost per user, etc).

2 *Checking lists* The strategy here is in determining the strengths and weaknesses of the collection by the comparison of appropriate lists to a list of the library's holdings. Such lists include: standard catalogues and basic general lists (eg *Books for college libraries, Choice's opening day collection*); catalogues of important libraries; specialised bibliographies and basic subject lists; current lists (best sellers, books of the year, etc); reference works (listed in standard guides); periodical lists (currently received, bound, listed in standard directories, etc); authorised lists (prepared by government authorities, professional association, etc); ad hoc lists (designed to meet the needs of a specific library or group of libraries citations (footnotes, bibliographies, in subjects of special interest to the library).

3 *Obtaining user opinion* The methods used consist of surveying individual users or groups of users in order to determine their personal evaluations on the strengths, weaknesses, effectiveness of the collection, by interview and/or questionnaire.

4 *Direct examination* The assessment of the collection in specific subject areas by some noted authority or expert, by direct examination at the shelf.

5 *Applying standards* The application of established standards or standards constructed from use of the methods discussed.

Bonn also describes two additional evaluation methods which are not specifically limited to a single collection: 1) 'rating total (internal and external) resource adequacy'; 2) 'document delivery capability'. In this discussion, the interdependability of libraries is recognised, and the need to evaluate individual libraries and groups as a whole. Document delivery capability has been the subject of statistical method study, and models fo measuring delivery capability are available. (8)

The advantages and disadvantages of each of the methods described by Bonn, and their appropriateness to the individual library, should be carefully examined before the adoption of one rather than another. The use of more than one method would seem to offer the best chance of accuracy, as the results could be compared.

The collection development policy

The collection development policy should be a document setting forth the broad objectives and principles of collection development in direct relationship with, and as a consequence of, the goals and objectives of the library and institution. The policy should include a general discussion of the nature, philosophy and constraints of collection development, and proceed to the specific identification of collection limits, strengths, weaknesses, and resource allocation on a departmental and subject basis. The procedures and mechanisms designed to facilitate the selection of library materials for acquisiton and de-acquisition should be clearly described, and should include clear descriptions of the functions of committees.

The policy should be shaped and adapted in accordance with the results indicated by the evaluation studies, which should be designed to monitor the performance of the policy at regular intervals. While it should be regarded as flexible and subject to modification as the need arises, the policy should clearly define the roles and responsibilities of those members of library staff and faculty involved in its operation. Where and when appropriate, the policy should be coordinated with other libraries or groups of libraries with a view to securing some measure of agreement in the development of cooperative approaches to collection development. To encourage and enable the comparison of policies between libraries, the American Library Association Collection Development Committee, Resources Section of the Resources and Technical Services Division, has defined levels of collection intensity, using what is hoped will be standard collecting intensity codes.

The code definitions consist of:

A   Comprehensive level. A collection in which a library endeavours . . to include all works of recorded knowledge . . .

B   Research level. A collection which includes the major source materials required for dissertations and independent research . . .

C   Study level. A collection which is adequate to support undergraduate or graduate course work, or sustained independent study . . .

D   Basic level. A highly selective collection which serves to introduce and define the subject and to indicate the varieties of information elsewhere . . .

E   Minimal level. A subject area which is out of scope for the library's collections, and in which few selections are made beyond very basic tools. (9)

While the application of these codes should occur in as objective a fashion as possible, some variability in interpretation seems inevitable. Nevertheless, clear definition of intensity levels is a valuable aid to the library user as well as to other libraries. The committee recommends that the codes be used in each subject to indicate: a) existing strength of the collection; b) current level of collecting activity; c) desirable level of

collecting. Other definitions for each subject category, consist of langua
codes, chronological periods and geographical areas collected, forms of
material collected, and identity of selector and/or selection unit. The
subject categories suggested by the committee, are the approximately
five hundred subdivisions used in *Titles classified by the Library of Congress Classification: seventeen university libraries* (preliminary edition,
Berkeley, General Library, University of California, 1973). The guidelines are concise, well-designed and provide a sound and consistent basis
for the collection development policy.

The process of book selection is approached by research libraries in
a variety of ways, usually depending upon the size and nature of the institution, and the number and expertise of library staff. Most academic
libraries have staff functioning in the role of subject specialists or bibliographers working with the academic departments and individual faculty
members on the selection process. The extent of faculty involvement
varies greatly from library to library and subject to subject. A great deal
is dependent upon: a) the standing of the library within the academic
community; b) the subject knowledge and bibliographical expertise of
the library staff; c) the interest and bibliographical expertise of the
faculty.

Clearly, the desirability to define the roles and responsibilities of libra
and faculty mentioned earlier, and the specificity of such definition, can
be variable. Changes in library staff and faculty can change the role of tl
bibliographer from subject specialist with wide decision-making power,
to mere library-faculty liaison with simple order processing duties. Libra
bibliographers must play a central role in the development of collection
development goals and objectives, the formulation of policy, and collection evaluation, and the collection development policy must state their
role as clearly as is practicable, especially in terms of policy review mechanisms.

The process of deselection as a means of enhancing the development
of the collection should be particularly emphasised in the policy. Library
staff and faculty have been accustomed over the years to 'acquisition
policies' and most seem familiar with the traditional book selection-for-
acquisition orientation of these policies. (10) The process should be
clearly described in terms of the application of the selection criteria cited
earlier, and should logically lead to any policies the library might have
regarding weeding.

An esssential, and often neglected, element of collection development
policy is the need to consider, and establish procedures to take into acco

the preservation needs of the library. In its broadest sense, the word 'preservation' conjures up the traditional responsibility of the research library 'to preserve the sum total of recorded human knowledge'. The discharge of this responsibility being clearly impossible for the individual library, has caused some libraries to diligently preserve a small slice of this sum total. Recent discussions by the Library of Congress, ARL Preservation of Research Library Materials Committee and others, aimed partly at the establishment of national and/or regional depositories for the preservation of at least one copy of all significant works as a part of a National Preservation Programme, could drastically alter even this role. In any event, the physical condition of library materials is a matter of great importance to the obligations and costs of collection maintenance, and to future availability and usability, and must therefore be a factor in selecting materials for purchase, storage or discard.

Weeding

The term 'weeding' has generally been applied to the activity of separating less useful items from the collection in order to enhance its effectiveness and to create space for newer, more useful items. The development of a 'working collection' in which browsing is not inhibited by less useful books is a natural consequence of weeding. (11) The validity of this statement is dependent upon the kinds of criteria used in identifying 'less useful', and on the assumption that browsing is enhanced by weeding. Carol Seymour,(12) and John Urquhart and J L Schofield (13) have each noted that they could find no studies to prove the enhancement of browsing by weeding, but argue that logically it must be true. Philip Morse, using such factors as 'interest span' and 'optimum collection size', presents a convincing argument that 'low-interest-potential' books do indeed inhibit browsing. (14)

The point is an important one, as weeding purely as a space-making activity is not normally regarded as a continuous process, and the amount of space an item consumes becomes a crucial criterion. Seymour is particularly concerned with aiding undergraduate browsing by weeding, and Howard McGaw points out the 'disastrous' effects on college students and to 'certain kinds of research' that the retention of outdated text books can have. (15) While J A and N C Urquhart (16) maintain that it is not known if or how the presence on the shelves of useless books distorts use, it seems clear that, as Buckland and Hindle (17) point out, a collection is 'biased' for the purposes of browsing by the unavailability of popular (more useful) books. In a curious reversal of this point,

Stanley Slote notes that one of the arguments against weeding is that it will destroy the 'integrity, unity, and overall design of the collection'. (1 Slote, in describing this argument as 'nonsense' confirms 'bias' by pointi out that unity and integrity are destroyed anyway in any collection that circulates.

Further arguments against weeding revolve around the concept of immediate and undifferentiated access to works of all periods, topics and scope, and the notion that, as no one can predict the future of currently unused materials they should remain available for serendipitous discovery. (19) Such arguments, while understandable and in some cases valid, become more unrealistic as collections grow. The disposition of ite weeded from the collection depend upon the strengths of these argumen against weeding, and the resources of the institution. Generally the opti consist of storage, replacement by micro-photographic means, exchange or sale, and discard. The success of any continuous selection activity, be in terms of the practical results and ready decision justification, lies in the establishment of clearly stated and easily understood criteria.

In the preceding discussion concerning collection development policy it was noted that selection criteria must be related to the stated objectiv of the institution and be affected by some continuous process of evaluation. Acquisition selection criteria are usually interpreted quite liberall by librarians (unless under severe financial constraints), most of the time the whole process of selection being a speculative activity based upon anticipated use. Weeding criteria can include the valuable elements of past use and experience which, when added to the objectives and criteria of the collection development policy, make up a more powerful manage ment tool. Paradoxically however, weeding is regarded as a much more hazardous undertaking than acquisition, possibly because of resistance to the use of statistical methods for evaluating patterns of use. While criter fall into two broad categories, objective and subjective, the methods mo: widely discussed in the literature have been statistical ones for determini patterns of use. In 1969, Jain noted that '. . . well over seven hundred studies of use of books, journals, and facilities . . .' had been published since 1900. (20)

The need for some studies to determine book use is rarely in dispute, but the degree of data production and reliability of purely statistical methods are frequently criticised. 'Those who apply [statistical method have the conviction that truth is mathematical, that it can be found only by counting.' lamented Stanley Pargellis. (21) In the thirty years since his statement, statistical methods, particularly the design and application of models, have become common. There are indications that models and data gathering have been misused, possibly in attempting too much specificity. Morse cautions that it is preferable to use a model requiring few data, with a known possible error rate of 25 per cent, than one '. . . which predicts with great accuracy but requires man-years of effort to acquire the data'. (22)

The misuse of Bradford's famous law and model prompted D J Urquhart to comment that '. . . Bradford's observations on the scatter of references among periodicals was a useful observation on the real world. But the more recent attempts at curve fitting in this field are good examples of the worst aspects of the academic approach'. (23)

I Objective criteria

Objective methods for weeding the collections fall into three general categories: a) statistical methods designed to measure and identify patterns of use; b) identification of materials by age, using either publication or accession date; c) identification of less useful materials by genre, type and/or form.

a) *Patterns of use* The rationale for weeding items by the frequency of types of use is that past use is a good indication of the extent of future use. The basic data used in determining past use are usually circulation records. All the methods used in determining patterns and frequency of use assume a close correlation between recorded use and unrecorded use. Probably the most complete study of use patterns was produced by Herman Fussler and Julian Simon, (24) and consists of a detailed examination of the relationships between records of past use and dates of publication, past use as an indicator of future use, and variations in patterns of use between materials of different characterisitics. Their basic conclusion was that, with certain qualifications, future use can be predicted on the basis of past use for groups of books with defined characteristics, and that objective, mechanical weeding guidelines are possible. Fussler, while noting that the average frequency of use in a large research collection may be as low as once in fifty years, cautions that use should not be used as the sole criterion, but points out that it is '. . . relevant to any alternative system of access that might provide several different levels of accessibility to research related materials.' (25)

Richard Trueswell's studies have indicated that the date of last circulation is possibly the best predictor of future use. (26) His basic criterion is to remove a book that has not circulated for seven years prior to current circulation.

A K Jain identifies two main methods for studying patterns of use; choosing a sample from the total collection and examining use over a lon period, or examining all books used during a specific time period. In addition to his review of prior studies, Jain discusses his method of 'relative use' which he claims incorporates all the advantages of the two basic methods, and also includes a method for identifying in-library use. (27)

The advantage of using past use as a basic weeding criterion is that it is a completely objective measure based upon a common set of data. Th increasing use of automated circulation systems in academic libraries would seem to encourage past-use weeding in the future. The disadvantage is the absolute dependence upon accurate circulation data covering quite a long period of time (seven years in the case of Trueswell's metho

b) *Identification by age* The rationale for weeding collections by applying cut-off limits to accession, copyright and publication dates, is that usefulness declines as age increases. In gross terms, the thesis has been tested and proved. Charles Gosnell maintains that the decline in use of ageing books (obsolescence) should be studied in a similar fashion to life insurance mortality tables which are not based upon '. . . infant deaths o the longevity of octogenarians but on these and all others of the population.' (28) S Bulick has attempted to construct a predictive model on aging versus use based upon use data over a five year period, which will indicate the point at which negligible use can be predicted. (29) Both Gosnell and Bulick use date of publication as the selection criterion. Stanley Slote discusses the uses and relative merits of publication, copyright, acquisition, and original publication dates, and date of rebinding, and notes that age data are often used as aids to subjective weeding decisions. (30) Philip Morse acknowledges the principle of ageing and wanin use, and that weeding by age can work fairly well for certain book classe but states, 'retirement by age retires some high potential [and perhaps high use] books simply because they are older, and leaves in the browsin collection too many low-potential books simply because they are young (31) A method of selection for weeding (to storage) using the date of cataloguing as the criterion is described by R Moss, who notes that this system was preferred because of late purchases of materials published earlier. (32)

c) *Identification by type* This method of weeding is concerned with the removal from the collection of groups of materials regarded as inappropr ate or less useful. Selection of these groups will depend upon the collection development policy of the institution, and will normally consist of materials regarded as being outside the scope of such policies. While it is recognised that fashions and patterns of research and teaching change, weeding by this method appears to be only an occasional, even finite, activity. The Yale book retirement study indicated that material could not be retired as a subject group en masse as every field checked included some heavily used books, and that specific titles were easier to weed than groups or types. (33) Certain kinds of materials of only ephemeral interest such as house newsletters, some yearbooks, etc, and duplicates of titles no longer in heavy demand, could be discarded on a continuous basis.

II Subjective criteria

The criteria used in selecting material for purchase, especially when identified in a collection development policy, usually provides the basis for subjective weeding decisions. The degree of specificity of the collection development policies will affect the kinds of weeding criteria used by the individual librarian and/or faculty member in making the decisions. Kraft notes that this kind of weeding is often done purely on the basis of 'subjective value' which identifies 'valuable' objects, the number of which 'is as limitless as are individual tastes and preferences', or on the basis of 'some ideal to which a community subscribes.' (34) Raymond Morris describes the weeding process as a matter of 'knowledge, judgement, and wisdom', and states that Yale could find few of their procedures that could be 'reduced to a formula or routine'. (35)

The Yale programme was initially designed to include active faculty participation in the at-the-shelf selection, but as the programme continued, it became clear that they could not maintain regular weeding time schedules. The Yale programme became solely dependent upon the selection judgement of librarians, the faculty monitoring selections through lists and shelf list cards. Ash points out that faculty selection is suspect anyway as they consider books solely in relationship to their narrow research interests, and are usually inexpert in the literature of their respective fields. (36) Wholly subjective selection decisions for weeding are difficult to defend when challenged, as 'knowledge, judgement, and wisdom' are attributes which are hard to prove and rarely accorded librarians by faculty. Usually value judgements include objective kinds of criteria such as publication date and evidence of use. The extent to which these quantifiable measures are regarded as factors depends upon the type of library and institution, and the clarity and specificity of the relevant policies.

III Serials weeding

While most of the methods used in weeding monographs apply to serials, certain other factors must be considered, and further strategies employed. Past use and publication dates are frequently used in combination to determine a weeding cut-off date which may be used to continuously weed serial runs. In cases where use date is not available, the incidence of references and citations in relationship to date may be used. A number of studies have indicated the strong relationship between the age and usefulness of serials, and formulae exist to aid in the identification of citation-use. (37) For citation-use data for a specific research library, journal citations may be analysed from the institution's works, such as faculty publications, graduate theses and dissertations. Other factors, such as cooperative periodical banks, and the availability of high-speed photocopy facilities, clearly play a part in serial weeding decisions.

IV Weeding policy

The weeding policy should be a document naturally developed from the collection development policy utilising identical basic criteria. Following a study to determine the most appropriate weeding criteria according to the purpose of the library, needs of the users and resources available, a set of standards and criteria should be established for each group of materials. The process of collection evaluation described earlier can be used initially in conjunction with other appropriate studies to help construct the criteria, and as a means thereafter of measuring the success of the policy. The disposition of weeded materials in terms of close-at-hand storage, remote storage, discard, etc, should be clearly stated. The procedures and mechanisms described in the collection development policy to facilitate acquisitions should be utilised in the weeding procedures. The different levels of access to library materials should be described and related to the weeding criteria. If possible, collection size limits for each mode of storage should be stated, and different or secondary levels of weeding described. Both collection development and weeding policies must be as specific as possible, and yet be flexible enough to permit changes as circumstances dictate.

Storage

The transfer of less useful books to some form of storage is a process designed to promote the best of both worlds. By discarding useless books and differentiating access by storage, it is possible to satisfy some of the space requirements for the addition of new books, and still protect the great cumulation of knowledge represented by little-used research material. Inevitably in time, weeding from storage must occur and/or more storage space, possibly by cooperation, must be found. A long range plan for storage is therefore a necessary and natural extension of the policies described earlier.

The most common response to the availability of storage space however, is to indulge in a 'fool's paradise' of delusion that such space is infinite, and to use storage as a device for avoiding discard decisions, and/or the crisis transfer of bulky materials. In such cases, usually at the beginning of a new library administration, a strong argument is often made that the library is approaching, or is at, a space crisis, and that either a new building or additional storage space must be created as a matter of urgency. This sense of urgency and crisis is sustained when storage space becomes available, and crisis weeding occurs. Crisis weeding uses shelf-consumption and some other factor (past use, value, etc) as equal criteria, large sets and long serial back-runs being relegated to storage because of the maximum shelf space gained with the minimum number of record changes. The short term effect is greatly beneficial, especially in terms of collection management, and the library continues spasmodically with the weeding 'policy'. Over a period of time however, the criteria balance subtly changes until shelf-consumption becomes the predominant consideration, large sets having moderate use being stored. As monographs are untouched by this process, the logical result is that moderately used sets are in storage, while totally unused and obsolete monographs are cluttering prime library space. It is at this point that real crisis occurs with high reader dissatisfaction and the dreary prospects of high cost solutions to the problems accumulated, often initiated, by some previous discredited administration. The scene is set for negotiations for more library buildings.

Storage should be used as a means of holding available portions of the collections which are potentially important for research appropriate to the institution, but which are not used frequently enough to justify a place on prime space shelves. There are two kinds of storage commonly used by academic libraries, close-at-hand storage and remote storage.

a) Close-at-hand storage

The storage of lesser used books either within the library or in some area immediately adjacent has many reassuring aspects to commend it. First is the ability to deliver books to the reader within a reasonably short period of time. Readers are less likely to be suspicious of weeding activities if the weeded books are at least within grasping distance.

Second, materials moved into close-at-hand storage purely on the basis of circulation data, can have all levels of use closely monitored in a closed-access system with a view to future second-level weeding. The data produced provides a much more cogent argument for discard or remote storage than circulation data alone.

95

Third, it is possible to permit some level of storage shelf access to qualified readers. While this seems to indicate excessive caution in a demonstrated low use area, there may be circumstances when reader access to a large set may be advisable.

Fourth, selection for storage at the point of acquisition is more easily facilitated, particularly in the case of donated research materials of anticipated low use.

The greater utilisation of space permitted by the storage concept is a major factor in considering the costs of record changing. Most close-at-hand storage occurs within buildings not designed for modern mechanical compact storage systems, so most of the shelving strategies employed have involved the use of conventional shelving. In closed access systems, this has usually involved classifying books by size and according simple list numbers. (38) In open or limited access storage systems, other methods of compacting books are used. Lucinda Conger describes a six size system within subject classification used in the Annex Library at Princeton, (39) and R Moss describes a non-size 'time-factor' classification used at University College, Dublin, and Teesside Polytechnic. (40)

The most common response to increases in size, according to Mariann Cooper, is the creation of separate subject libraries. (41) Philip Morse claims that subject sub-division enhances browsing. (42) Given the premium value of space in, or close to the library however, it seems that this kind of decentralisation is probably too expensive, and that close-at-hand storage of lesser used materials is a more permanent response to size.

b) Remote storage

The chief argument for the use of storage facilities distant from the library is that used by Charles Eliot in 1902, namely that '. . . books very seldom used, should be stored in inexpensive buildings on cheap land.' (4 The advantage of such a plan is that a building can be specially construct for storage only, leaving space for expansion. Unfortunately, Eliot's stat ment is frequently taken literally to mean the acquisition of existing com mercial warehouse facilities without proper environmental controls, and often in dilapidated condition. Storing lesser used, but apparently neces sary, research materials in these circumstances is understandably often m with great resistance. In addition, delivery time is likely to be long, and relegation from this form of storage is almost certain to mean discard.

Off-campus storage however, is likely to be an increasingly more pop response to the problems of shrinking space, both as an individual library enterprise and as a cooperative venture between libraries. The most prom ising direction seems to be toward cooperative storage centres. Joanne

Harrar, in her review of some of the characteristics of cooperative storage (44), notes that traditionally, one form of cooperative activity seems bound to others. Thus in the case of cooperative storage:

mutually acceptable criteria for selection and deposit of little-used material, cooperative acquisitions even cooperative special-isation in collecting have been considered by storage proponents thus broadening—and complicating—the scope of activity.

The complicated nature of these related activities and other factors (such as legal ownership problems, proprietory attitudes and bibliographic control difficulties), are probably responsible for the fact that Harrar could identify only three cooperative storage enterprises 'of appreciable scale' in the United States. Increasing automation of bibliographic processes will remove some of the barriers to cooperation, and encourage both the sharing of resources and the establishment of cooperative storage facilities.

Preservation

The term 'preservation' is used here to refer to all processes and conditions designed to preserve knowledge, including conservation (binding, restoration, de-acidification, etc), reprography (micro-photography, photocopy, etc), storage conditions (environmental control, shelving mode, etc). The physical condition and format of library materials, and the preservation resources available to the library, are important factors for consideration in collection development and weeding decisions. For example, the existence of commercial micro-film or in-library filming facilities is often the deciding factor in the discard decision for a work in poor condition. In a sense, a library's collection development policies are directly concerned with preservation, as the library has a responsibility to preserve what is collected, therefore the costs of this preservation help determine what is collected, what is discarded and what is retained.

By the same token, the problems of coordinating collection development activities among libraries, are identical to the problems of preservation co-ordination. A library chooses to preserve only a slice of knowledge under its care, and chooses not to preserve (sometimes discard) the other slices. There are serious problems in trying to prevent each library from preserving identical slices at high cost and from discarding identical slices at great loss. At a recent planning conference for a US national preservation programme, Warren Haas noted that what must be developed within the next five to ten years are: a master negative film collection; centralised cold storage; a bibliographic control system capable of accepting film format. (45) Centralised cold storage for preservation purposes is the concept of storing, as a national responsibility, a single copy of every book in a centralised (national or regional) facility. (46)

Haas further remarked upon the urgent need for training programmes to provide research libraries with some staff trained in preservation techniques. Some libraries may be resistant to the notion of hiring trained preservation staff on the grounds of expense. A recent Association of Research Libraries, Office of University Library Management Studies survey indicated that from a surveyed group of forty-eight research libra only six had a plan or programme for the preservation of library materia and only six had a staff member assigned the specific tasks of conservati planning, collection maintenance and environmental controls (thirty-one libraries believed that such a staff member was needed). The libraries surveyed each spent an average of 171,350 dollars in fiscal year 1976-77 on preservation (47) The scale of these costs would seem to indicate the need for cooperative preservation action, and suggests the desirability of resource planning.

Steady-state

The term steady-state is a less negative, and happily, more ambiguous way of saying zero growth. The steady-state concept is that of the 'ever normal-granary' (48); acquisition and discarding of books should be balanced to maintain a collection at a steady state in terms of numbers of volumes. Attitudes to steady-state vary according to type of instituti and size of library collection. In general, the more research-orientated t institution and larger the library, the greater the opposition to the notio Conversely, the less an institution is involved in non-curricular research, and the smaller and more specific the library collection, the greater the advocacy of steady-state. It appears, paradoxically, that the larger the li brary the greater the reluctance to control growth, the smaller the librar the greater the enthusiasm for growth control. Librarians of smaller libraries seem to take delight in gibing at the 'Towers of Babel' represente by the perpetuators of Alexandria, and claim that solutions to library obesity are easy to implement. (49) Librarians of large research librarie may typically respond that it is all very well for the college librarian to proclaim the discovery of steady-state at the same time sending his researchers off to the obese research library down the street.

As a comprehensive activity, it seems that the smaller and more speci the collection, the easier it is to make decisions about its future. Acqui- sition, collection evaluation, weeding, record adjustment, are here simpl less expensive activities. Identification of under-used books and heavily-used books is easier as they are fewer, and in fewer disciplines. Even wholly subjective weeding approaches are possible in some cases. (50) Large research collections are not merely multiplications of small collections, the higher cost factor for record adjustment, evaluation and selection is not simply a matter of increased scale. Most large research libraries face a set of complex issues quite outside the normal activities of the smaller college library. The great emphasis placed upon research and the compelling and exacting requirements made by faculty, responsibility for the preservation of unique collections, the reliance of small libraries, are burdens more likely to be carried by the large research library than the college library. These differences however, do not completely invalidate the concept of stady-state for the research library, but indicate that a modified approach is necessary.

Steady-state as a partial activity would seem to be an appropriate and flexible response to growth by the research library. The partial steady-state strategy could consist of the following three kinds of activities: a) comprehensive steady-state strategies in selected areas; b) development of working collection by means of differentiated access; c) promotion of cooperative approaches to collection development and preservation;

a) *Selective steady-state* Portions of the collection characteristically subject to fast ageing, such as text books, manuals, and certain periodicals, should be identified as a group and subjected to the rigours of steady-state. Circulation data should be used as basic evidence of use, preferably employing Trueswell's 'shelf-time period' as the method of selection. Duplication of heavily-used books should occur based upon the same method.

b) *Development of a working collection* Books readily available and consuming premium space should justify their place in terms of use. The concept of a working collection should be developed by assigning use criteria to the total collection and dividing it into different levels of access. The optimum size for the working collection should be established, and lesser-used books relegated to close-at-hand storage. Ideally, such storage should be closed to readers, an optimum size set, and use and other kinds of criteria applied to the storage collection for possible relegation to remote storage. (51) Remote storage may be an off-campus, environmentally-controlled warehouse for the use of one library, or a cooperative resource-sharing depository such as Center for Research Libraries, or a combination. The storing of rarely-used materials is appropriate for remote storage.

c) *Cooperative approaches* The creation of regional or national resource centres where rare, esoteric, and little-used materials are stored and made available, seems a vitally important development for the future. In the meantime, the initiative for cooperative approaches to collection develop ment and preservation must come from individual research libraries. The accelerating trend towards automation has encouraging implications for these cooperative approaches. The rapid growth in the use and applicatio of OCLC (52) for example, has made possible faster access to book locat information. Fussler warned that as a consequence of the size and inflex bility of card catalogues, some research libraries may seek new alternativ (53) Since Fussler's prediction, the Library of Congress has announced t closing of its card catalogue in 1980, and the development of an on-line automated catalogue. Many research libraries are considering following the Library of Congress lead. The present high level of costs likely to be involved in the continuous movement and status change records neces- sary to the steady-state concept, is certain to be greatly reduced by the u of computers. If these high costs have inhibited growth stabilisation in the past, there should be every expectation that significant cost reductio will promote growth stabilisation.

Trends at Johns Hopkins University

The Milton S Eisenhower Library is the largest library of Johns Hopk University, and the only library on the Homewood campus. (54) The building was opened in 1965, but by 1974 it was practically full. The collection presently stands at roughly two million titles. In the early par of 1974 a new administration, with the help of staff task forces, identifi the major problems confronting the library as: lack of space; lack of coherent collection development procedures; lack of basic data. Althou library funds were low, planning began for identifying and storing lesser- used books in the old Gilman Library stacks, and the upgrading of envir mental conditions. Between the summer of 1974 and the winter of 197 five major steps had been taken to rectify some of the deficiencies: a) a collection development programme was initiated; b) the library joined t Ohio College Library Center (OCLC); c) a fully automated circulation system was installed; d) identification and storage of less-used books began; e) physical preservation of the collection began.

a) *Collection development programme* The programme was develop in order to identify the most effective means of enhancing the collectio to make the most efficient use of available space; and to help determine which items in the collection should be preserved in original form, whic should be replaced in some other form, and which should be discarded. Twenty librarians were assigned specific subject areas on the basis of the subject knowledge and bibliographical expertise. These collection development librarians began the task of shaping the collections, maintaining communication with academic departments through twenty-nine faculty 'department liaison officers'. As each collection development librarian had other library duties, a collection development center was established to coordinate activities, provide special search capabilities, and to become a base for gift receipts. Collection development policies are presently in the process of formulation by the CDL's as a result of the activities of the center.

b) *Ohio College Library Center* Towards the end of 1974, the library became an active member of OCLC, which made several technical processing improvements possible, speeding up cataloguing, standardising procedures and giving updated holdings and location information. The full potential of the system has not yet been realised, and there seems to be great promise of further collection development applications.

c) *Computer Library Systems, Inc (CLSI) LIBS-100 Circulation System* The decision to install the system was based on the former system's high recurring costs, the error potential of the microfilm/keypunch process, the time-lag in updating the circulation file print-out, and the inadequacy of the data. The CLSI system provides fully-automated, on-line access to circulation records, produces overdues and other notices, and generates meaningful circulation data for any time period, and/or title. The system will prove more valuable as the depth of data increases, and will be a vital tool in applying collection development and weeding criteria.

d) *Storage of lesser-used books* The need to quickly create space was the over-riding consideration in the initial stages of the storage programme. In 1976, the librarian reported that between 1400 and 1600 shelves of materials were being added to the collection every year, the most recent additions consisting of five hundred shelves of bound periodicals, two hundred shelves of documents, and 822 shelves of books. By June 1976 only five hundred empty shelves remained in the Eisenhower building, and few of these were located in the right places. The response to this crisis was to begin storage of lesser-used journal runs, as this created the maximum amount of shelf space with the minimum number of record changes. The breathing space thus created is enabling a rational appraisal of weeding and storing procedures which, along with the transfer of low-use research materials for cooperative storage to the Center for Research Libraries, and investigations into the feasibility of regional cooperative storage and resource sharing, promises a greater measure of growth control.

101

e) *Preservation* Early in 1975, planning was initiated for a major attack upon the library's preservation problems, preliminary investigatic revealing the roughly tripartite nature of the problems—binding of curre receipts; care for the research collection; replacement of materials too deteriorated for practical restoration.

The binding of current receipts, mainly journal binding, was the mos expensive portion of the preservation budget, and was thus the first are. of enquiry. Roughly 15,000 periodical titles were bound annually to identical standards, a fact which prompted four separate surveys of use-after-binding. As most bound periodicals at the Eisenhower Library are permitted to circulate, it was decided that times circulated and evidence of use and evidence of wear, would provide the basis for data gathering. With the exclusion of twenty known high-use abstracts and indexes, it was discovered that most bound periodicals circulate very infrequently and show very little evidence of use and wear. Based upon the results o the surveys, a binding was designed based on the following criteria: low cost; reversible (to permit rebinding, should unforeseen future heavy us require it); opening flat (to facilitate photocopy and/or microfilm); per mitting fore-edge shelving without structural damage (to facilitate possi compact storage). Rigid specifications were designed and bids from cor mercial book-binders invited. After two years careful monitoring, the results have been highly satisfactory, not a single binding showing signs of failing and with a current sixty per cent cost saving on 1975 binding costs.

In order to upgrade the condition of the permanent parts of the rese collection, a restoration bindery was established on pragmatic lines designed to examine and treat a wide variety of materials. As training for conservation is non-existent in the United States, an extensive training programme was devised based upon a traditional apprenticeship model. The bindery is the first phase in a preservation strategy designed to incl paper restoration and filming units.

The existence of restoration facilities requires that a critical selectio for-treatment process take place. In this respect, the combined capabil ties of collection development librarians and circulation staff help prov the necessary data to enable decisions on replacement (by reprint, film, photocopy), rebinding (relevance to collection, extent of use), restorati (bibliographical importance, value), and discard. A continuing refurbis ing and examination of the collections at the shelf encourages these decisions, particularly in terms of weeding-for-discard, as a decision not to weed an item in poor condition, incurs a known replacement, rebinding or restoration cost.

102

Activities of the last three years have also included the establishment of an information retrieval division (to provide on-line access to most science, social science, business, education, and psychology data bases), and the completion of a one year staff study of management processes under the ARL Management Review and Analysis Program. While much remains to be accomplished at the Eisenhower Library to control growth, enhance collection use, and gain access to a greater depth of information resources, the vigorous steps taken thus far have provided a strong base for future developments.

Conclusion

The concept of balancing the number of incoming books exactly with the number of outgoing books is not as simple as many of the more avid advocates of steady-state appear to claim. Not enough is known about the complex processes of individual research, or about the future role of machines. Probable developments toward the establishment of on-line catalogues, the standardisation of collection development and weeding procedures, the creation of national/regional resource centers, the establishment of a national preservation programme, possibly even agreements by researchers to limit or centralise their research requirements, will all combine to greatly slow down collection growth trends.

Many research libraries are already facing the unpalatable reality that library building expansion cannot continue, and alternatives to expansion are being realistically sought. It seems likely that the steady-state concept will spread, but will be applied in a variety of ways. Special libraries and small teaching collection libraries will be able to rigorously weed the under-used, outdated, and unfashionable, while research libraries will always be faced with the onerous responsibility to preserve materials likely to be needed for research. The purely quantitative approach to acquisition and weeding may be applied to small specific collections, whether a complete teaching collection or a well-identified portion of a large research collection. The larger and more complex the collection, the greater the variety of growth control strategies that must be applied.

In the final analysis, steady-state and growth control is a state of mind, a necessary realisation by librarians that the 'extra' time and cost burden placed upon them by weeding/discard/storage decision making has become basic to librarianship, and is not extra at all.

REFERENCES

1   Marianne Cooper 'Criteria for weeding of collections' *Library resources and technical services* 12 (3), summer 1968, 339-351.

O C Dunn, W F Seibert and Janice A Scheuneman *The past and likely future of 58 research libraries 1951-1980: a statistical study of growth and change* Lafayette, Indiana, Purdue University, 1965.

Herman H Fussler *Research libraries and technology* Chicago, Universi of Chicago Press, 1973.

Claudia Schorrig 'Sizing up the space problem in academic libraries' *Farewell to Alexandria* ed Daniel Gore. Westport, Connecticut, Greenwood Press, 1976, 6-21.

These works collectively present a comprehensive analysis of the phenor ena of library growth. The latter work by Claudia Schorrig provides a detailed study and analysis of space problems, and includes some useful statistics.

2 Margit Kraft 'An argument for selectivity in the acquisitions of m terials for research libraries' *Library trends* 37 (3), July 1967, 284-295 Argues that some measure of control is in the hands of the librarian as t 'only answer to indiscriminate publishing is increasingly selective buyin Daniel Gore 'The view from the Tower of Babel' *Library journal* 100, Sept 1975, 1599-1605. Appears to endorse José Ortega y Gasset's view that in the future librarians should be 'held responsible by society for th regulation of the production of books'.

3 B J Enright 'Biblioclothanasia: library hygiene and the librarian' *Essays on information and libraries* eds Keith Barr and Maurice Line, London, Bingley; Hamden, Conn, Linnet, 1975, 70.

4 Ibid, 68.

5 Claudia Schorrig, op cit.

6 Michael K Buckland and Anthony Hindle 'Acquisitions, growth and performance control through systems analysis' *Farewell to Alexan* 50.

7 George S Bonn 'Evaluation of the collection' *Library trends* 22 Jan 1974, 265-304.

8 Bonn cites Richard H Orr et al 'Development of methodologic tools for planning and managing library services: II measuring a library' capability for providing documents' *Bulletin of the Medical Library Association* 60, July 1972, 382-422.

9 Collection Development Committee, Resources Section, Resourc and Technical Services Division, 'ALA guidelines for the formulation of collection development policies', *Library resources and technical servic* 21 (1), winter 1977, 40-47.

10 Louis Round Wilson and Maurice F Tauber *The university librar* New York, Columbia University Press, 1956. In their section 'Book

collections: acquisition policies and procedures' (chapter IX and subsequent chapters X and XI), the authors provide a well argued and detailed framework for such a policy.

11 Barbara A Rice 'The development of working collections in university libraries' *College and research libraries* 38 (4), July 1977, 309-312. Provides a short overview of this topic.

12 Carol Seymour 'Weeding the collections' *Libri* 22 (2), 1972, 138.

13 John Urquhart and J L Schofield 'Measuring readers' failure at the shelf in three university libraries' *Journal of documentation* 28 (3), Sept 1972, 233-241.

14 Philip M Morse 'Measures of library effectiveness' *Operations research implications for libraries* Chicago, University of Chicago Press, 1972, 399.

15 Howard F McGaw 'Policies and practices in discarding' *Library trends* 4 (3), Jan 1956, 269-282.

16 J A Urquhart and N C Urquhart *Relegation and stock control in libraries* Stocksfield, Oriel Press, 1976, 36.

17 Buckland and Hindle, op cit.

18 Stanley J Slote *Weeding library collections* Littleton, Colorado, Libraries Unlimited, 1975, 6.

19 Margit Kraft (op cit) notes that the argument for retaining less useful or unused materials because of an inability to predict future use is often forgotten when selection for purchase occurs, as material is usually selected on the basis of potential use. She points out that 'a large amount of the material accumulated for future use has never been used and may never be used.' 290.

20 A K Jain 'Sampling and data collection methods for a book-use study' *Library quarterly* 39 (3), July 1969, 245.

21 Stanley Pargellis 'Building a research library' *College and research libraries* 5, March 1944, 112.

22 Philip Morse, op cit, 20.

23 D J Urquhart 'Looking backwards and forwards' *Aslib proceedings* 27 (6), June 1975, 232.

24 Herman H Fussler and Julian L Simon *Patterns in the use of books in large research libraries* Chicago, University of Chicago Press, 1969.

25 Fussler *Research libraries and technology* op cit, 23.

26 Richard W Trueswell 'A quantitative measure of user circulation requirements and its possible effect on stack thinning and multiple copy determination' *American documentation* 16, Jan 1965, 20-25. Trueswell has written extensively on this topic, his most recent work published to

date being his 'Growing libraries: who needs them? A statistical basis for the no-growth collection', in *Farewell to Alexandria.*

27 A K Jain, op cit, 245.

28 Charles F Gosnell, 'Obsolescence of books in college libraries' *College and research libraries* 5 (2), March 1944, 116.

29 S Bulick 'Use of library materials in terms of age' *American Soci of Information Science Journal* 27, May 1976, 175-178.

30 Stanley Slote, op cit, 35-36. Slote recommends a method which i a product of past use study, 'shelf-time period' which uses as criterion the period between circulations.

31 Philip M Morse 'Search theory and browsing' *Library quarterly* 40 (4), Oct 1970, 408.

32 R Moss 'Time factor classification' *Aslib proceedings* 27, June 1975, 273-277.

33 Lee M Ash *Yale's selective book retirement program* Hamden, Conn, Archon Books, 1963, 8-10.

34 Margit Kraft, op cit, 287.

35 Lee M Ash, op cit, 66.

36 Ibid, 9-13. Less than 5 per cent of a faculty of 177 (100 in the humanities, and 77 in the social sciences) had received training in their respective literature.

37 Carol Seymour 'Weeding the collection: a review of research on identifying obsolete stock. Part II: Serials' *Libri* 22 (3), 1972, 183-189 A review of some of the studies to date.

38 Lee M Ash, op cit. Describes the Yale system of size classificatio Manuel D Lopez 'Compact book storage: solutions utilising conventiona methods' *Library trends* 19 (3), Jan 1971, 352-361. Presents a review of systems in general use.

39 Lucinda Conger 'The annex library of Princeton University: the development of a compact storage library' *College and research libraries* 31, March 1970, 160-168.

40 R Moss, op cit. Claims that this system avoids the need for recor changing. Briefly the strategy is to automatically relegate to storage on the basis of cataloguing date which is added to the call number, differen time factors being used for different disciplines.

41 Cooper, op cit, 340.

42 Morse, op cit, 391.

43 Charles William Eliot 'The division of a library into books in use, and books not in use, with different storage methods for the classes of books' *Library journal* 27, June 1902, 53.

R E Ellsworth *The economics of book storage in college and university libraries* Metuchen, N J, ARL and Scarecrow Press.
H J Harrar, 'Cooperative storage' *Library trends* 19, Jan 1971, 318-328.
Both Ellsworth and Harrar indicate that remote storage should not be regarded as a cheap alternative to in-library storage as Eliot appeared to suggest. Ellsworth is 'unenthusiastic' about so-called cost advantages because of record-changing costs and the 'possible alienation of faculty', while Harrar notes that 'cooperative storage warehouses' do not make economies, but in some cases 'extend resources'.

44 H Joanne Harrar, ibid, 318.

45 *Library of Congress information bulletin* Feb 1977.

46 There has been some disagreement as to the form of the book stored (de-acidified original or film), but the idea of 'national resource copies' from which copies could be made on demand is generally accepted in principle.

47 ARL, Office of University Library Management Studies, 'Collection analysis project survey: preservation of library materials' Unpublished survey of October 1977.

48 Lee M Ash, op cit, 14-15.

49 Daniel Gore, 'Farewell to Alexandria: the theory of the no-growth high-performance library' in *Farewell to Alexandria*, op cit, 164-180. And 'The view from the Tower of Babel' *Library journal* 100, 15 Sept 1975, 1599-1605.

50 Ray Prytherch and Claire Anderson 'Book retirement' *New library world* 77, March 1976, 49-51. The authors note their success in reducing collection size by 6.6 per cent over a four year period despite an annual acquisitions rate of 16.6 per cent, using mainly subjective weeding techniques. The collection consists of only 15,000 volumes in an 'independent departmental library' of Leeds Polytechnic.

51 The value of close-at-hand storage as a staging area has been recognised by many. B J Enright in his 'Biblioclothanasia' notes that 'it seems essential to organise a system where material under threat of retirement can linger for a cooling off period' (75) Even with the 15,000 volume library 'no-growth' system noted by Prytherch and Anderson, it was found necessary to employ such an area 'whereby books are weeded after a further two years'. (51).

52 The Ohio College Library Center is an automated, inter-active cataloguing system.

53 Herman Fussler *Research libraries and technology*, op cit, 26.

54 Other libraries of the university include the Welch Medical Library, the Library of the School of Advanced International Studies, and the Applied Physics Laboratory Library.

STEADY-STATE AND LIBRARY COOPERATION

Bernard Naylor

Growth and cooperation: some preliminary considerations

IN THE GROWTH and development of large libraries, the relationship
between capital and recurrent expenditure is inextricably complex, and
the distinction between them, it can be argued, is often only one of administrative convenience, however firmly made. Capital expenditure is
traditionally seen, at least in the case of academic libraries in the United
Kingdom, as a term covering the occasional allocation of very large sums
of money to meet the library's space requirements. Recurrent expenditure
is the regular disbursement carried on by the library to maintain its staffing
commitments, its book, monograph and serial acquisitions, its binding
programme and so on.

At any given point in time, a library's stock of books and periodicals,
acquired by recurrent expenditure over a long period of years is rightly
regarded as a valuable capital asset, both of the library itself and of the
parent institution. It has indeed been argued that expenditure on acquisitions is capital expenditure (1). Although in the course of time they can
become worn out, library materials are customarily used, yet not used up.
There are also occasions when libraries receive exceptional allocations
to enable them to establish new collections. This may be in recognition
of the need to support a newly established academic course, or may result
from a conscious decision by the parent body or another funding institution
to establish in one library a pre-eminent stock in some subject field. Allocations of this kind bear an even closer resemblance to capital grants as
customarily regarded.

When the activities of a large academic library are closely examined, it
can be seen that the establishment of steady-state in one part of the organism
does not mean that the whole attains a steady-state in harmony with it.
If a library's book fund is kept at the same level in real terms, the acquisitions and cataloguing programmes will be similarly stabilised. However,
the collection will continue to grow and therefore to require periodic

109

inputs of capital expenditure to provide more space, increased staff to service the larger collection, if the reader's ease of access is to be maintained, and possibly increased effort to manage the larger and correspondingly more complex catalogue. Alternatively, at some stage, the limit of the library's existing capacity will be reached, and expense will have to be incurred in outhousing or relegating those materials for which on-site space can no longer be provided. The library's acquisition and cataloguing programme may then also have to be modified, perhaps severely, so that it can be brought into balance with a stock relegation programme.

On the face of it, it ought apparently to be possible to achieve just such a state of equilibrium, one in which the resources allocated to book and serials purchase, cataloguing, stock relegation and catalogue weeding are in balance, and all contained within the stable space allocation accorde to the library. From the service point of view, however, the library exists to place its user in contact with the literature he or she comes there to consult. Whatever the stability achieved within the library, outside it the growth of the corpus of the written word continues. Ashworth has argued that the useful corpus remains roughly the same in size. (2) The majority of voices claim, like Renaissance man, that if today we have achieved a more distant vision, it is only because we stand (intellectually speaking) on the shoulders of previous generations, and that in practical experience, while the frontiers of knowledge expand the hinterland does not fold up neatly behind. Within his stable environment, therefore, the librarian is likely to experience a diminishing capability to meet his readers' needs, and, since that is his ultimate raison d'être, it is fair to ask what kind of stability it is he has achieved.

It might be possible to consider separately the effects of imposing stability (but at what level?) in each of the different aspects of a library's activities and to follow the repercussions through the system. As applied to academic libraries, however, steady-state is usually taken to refer to the physical size of the collection, and that is how it will be principally understood for the remainder of this chapter. But as the argument already advanced is meant to illustrate, the imposition of a total restriction on growth will require a modification to those programmes maintained by the library as it grew to the 'optimum' level chosen, and will also carry implications for the library's ability to meet the expectations of its users. So the physical size of the collection cannot and will not be considered in total isolation.

Historically, cooperation between academic libraries long predates the concept of the steady-state library. Underlying the establishment of mode of cooperation is an appreciation that it is at best inappropriate and at worst impossible for every library to attempt to put itself in a position to satisfy every conceivable reader requirement. It may be thought inappropriate because at some stage the investment required to achieve a higher level of reader satisfaction is judged disproportionate when the significance of the reader's satisfaction proves to be marginal or irrelevant to the institution's purposes. It may be thought impossible because long before reaching the stage of considering the possibility of satisfying the reader's marginal requirements, the institution's financial resources reach their limit, and some other way has to be found of giving the reader access to what the institution accepts he has a need for.

The question of the appropriateness of a given level of provision has received increasingly concentrated attention in recent years, exemplified by the formulation of what has been called the 80-20 rule. (3) Eighty per cent of the use of an academic library has, in certain instances, been found to focus on 20 per cent of the stock. The bald statement needs some clarification.

The aspect of library use which is most easily assessed is borrowing. Since some materials, such as essential and heavily used bibliographic works, are commonly designated 'reference use only', use studies frequently take no account of them. They also often fail to take account of in-library use of library materials which the user happens to prefer to consult in the library rather than to take away. However, such studies as have been done appear to suggest that adding in-library use to the statistics of use by borrowers does not radically alter the general impression of a concentration of use on a small portion of stock. (4) In order to satisfy the demands of his readers, the librarian does not need an inordinate extra stock. However, in order *to be sure* of satisfying it from material in stock, the librarian would have no alternative but to acquire everything, since he has no way of knowing for sure what the residual demand will be for. Since this is manifestly impossible, the solution is to plan the use of financial resources in such a way that the librarian achieves from stock as high a level of reader satisfaction as possible. But for the remainder he is dependent on outside resources, possibly on some form of cooperative arrangement. And if the size of his library is fixed, and the corpus of literature growing, he is likely to encounter a declining rate of user satisfaction.

In order to facilitate the discussion of different aspects of library cooperation and to relate this discussion to the interactive process within the library, I should like to identify some factors which are important in assessing the significance of any scheme of cooperation and the extent to which it impinges on a participant library's internal processes and financial arrangements.

Autonomy, jealously guarded by librarians, constitutes the right to use available resources in satisfying the library's own clientele. Although libraries must clearly depend on many outside facilities for normal functioning (post, telephone, electricity, and, in the final analysis, other libraries), there is, in respect of books and periodicals, an understandable feeling that if readers' needs are known sufficiently well in advance, they ought to be met from the library's own stock. Librarians may therefore be inhibited from reaching agreements on cooperation since their obligatio is first to serve the staff and students of their own institution, and any agreement which would have the effect of reducing the allocation given to that priority can probably not be entertained.

In the course of participating in a scheme of library cooperation, a library may incur specific *costs*, an identifiable element of expenditure in its budget devoted to the pursuit of cooperative aims. Costs may be incurred in the purchase of special materials in accordance with a scheme for cooperation. They may arise from the extra expenditure required by a union or shared cataloguing activity (though the latter is more commonl argued for on the ground of cost savings). They may be incurred in such service to readers as enhanced inter-library loan systems, improved telecommunications etc. If the library's budget cannot be increased proportionately, such costs inevitably have the effect of reducing the resource available for other activities. However, they are not necessarily associated with a permanent reduction in autonomy, unless there is at the same time some commitment to continue participating in a particular cooperative activity. Libraries' attitudes to expenditure can be indicative of their attitudes towards a particular mode of cooperation. For example, if their resources are sufficient they may be prepared to spend money rather than to incur some loss of autonomy or increased internal costs, for example in staff time. Financial stringency, however, can exert pressure to modify this attitude.

All forms of library cooperation require a basis of *information*. It is un wise to send a reader to another library unless there is good reason to expect that he will find there the material he wants to consult. Informatic about another library's holdings may be derived from personal acquaintan and if so may not always be written down. But it is more likely to be derived from a printed source.

Such a printed source may be general in character (a directory or guide to resources) or specific (a catalogue). It may be devoted to the resources of one library or of several brought together because of their common relevance to a theme. The effort involved in producing it may have been expended principally to further the purposes of one institution, as for example when the catalogue of a collection is published in order to make a collection or library more widely known. Or it may be produced specifically to further inter-library use and inter-library cooperation.

In the process of gathering and distributing information, libraries are likely to incur costs. But they need not necessarily lose autonomy. True, the information gathered may refer to commitments entered into by the library, which have the effect of restricting its autonomy, and if these exist, it may be helpful to publicise them. But many libraries which publicise their collections and services still retain entire freedom of action within the scope afforded by their budget.

Protocols is a term to refer to the agreements reached between libraries and intended to further cooperation. These range extremely widely and may cover arrangements for acquisitions, cataloguing or reader services. The information sources I have described may usefully record protocols and protocols may constitute the prior agreement which lead to the preparation of such information sources.

Protocols do not necessarily involve the library in extra costs, though they often do. Nor do they necessarily imply loss of autonomy. A library may adhere to a protocol which simply proclaims an arrangement which is part of the library's declared policy anyway. But one of the crucial criteria libraries in effect use when deciding whether they wish to adhere to a particular protocol is what effect it has on their costs and on their autonomy. Their attitudes here are a significant yardstick, it will be argued later, in demonstrating their general attitude to cooperation.

Machinery is a term to describe the procedures by which an on-going cooperative activity is maintained. Machinery may actually consist of machinery, for example computer hardware—and its attendant staff—required to produce and maintain a union catalogue. Machinery also means the processes of consultation and decision-making often established to further cooperation between libraries. Protocols may in fact require the establishment of machinery to implement or monitor some agreement. Machinery may also be closely linked with information. It may be necessary for the proper consideration of the information gathered and the process of taking decisions (and possibly making protocols) based upon it.

Machinery needs money—for staff, for equipment, possibly for travel and associated secretarial expenses—if it is to be maintained and continued.

113

It also clearly implies a loss of autonomy, in the sense that it requires library personnel to become involved with activities not wholly contained within the library on a continuous and committed basis.

Having put forward some preliminary considerations both about the concept of a steady-state library, and also about library cooperation, I now want to look briefly at the history, present state and future prospect of library cooperation, with these factors in mind. Although my approach will continue to assume that the steady-state library is principally characterised by a rigid limit on space provision, it should be remembered that this concept is intricately and inextricably linked with other aspects of library management and library provision. It should also be remembered that there is an equally complex relationship between the different aspects of library cooperation I have so far touched on.

Inter-library use

The US national inter-library loan code of 1968 has defined inter-library loans as 'Transactions in which library materials are made available by one library to another for the use of an individual.' Expressed in this way, it becomes clear that bringing the book to the reader is simply an alternative (historically a later alternative) to sending the reader to the book. The history of the wandering scholar is very ancient. Initially, no doubt, librarians relied on their own specialised knowledge and later, on the published catalogues of other libraries if they wanted to know at which library a desired book might be read. Nowadays the reference librarian has an array of published union catalogues (especially of periodicals) and guides to resources to help him and he can usually call on centralised services such as the *National union catalog* in the United States or the union catalogues of the British Library Lending Division. This indicates that in its original expression, library cooperation grew from an attitude of mind amongst librarians, a readiness to show hospitality to readers who had genuine enquiries and were unable to satisfy their needs in the library to which they first resorted. As Davey has said 'Library cooperation is built upon the pride in helping one's neighbours.' (5)

For a reader to resort to another library is prima facie evidence that the resources of the first library are insufficient. Libraries themselves, however, have not necessarily always regarded this as proof of the inadequacy of their own service. So far as they are concerned, the level of expenditure required to meet all such needs would be inappropriate for the fundamental functions they are trying to perform.

Let us now measure this first type of 'cooperation' against the considerations discussed earlier. Any costs involved are usually incurred by

114

the reader. The library's autonomy is not affected. There is little or no machinery involved, except possibly a standardised form of introduction as exemplified at present by the SCONUL vacation reading ticket, or the University of London inter-library day ticket. Protocols are not usually required, except for the implementation of any necessary machinery. The information which enables the reader to turn to another collection may be of the most elementary kind, though it may be the outcome of a significant piece of work by one individual or by library staff collaborating (in which case, of course, there will be costs involved). It can therefore be readily seen that this type of cooperation, if it can even be properly so called, has never been looked to by libraries as an alternative to on-site provision and has therefore had no implications for steady-state, whether narrowly or broadly construed. But it is an essential feature of many, more far-reaching schemes of cooperation, and therefore serves as a preliminary sign of any library's readiness to engage in more extended cooperative schemes.

Though able to utilise the collections of other libraries by sending readers to them, libraries have clearly felt an increasing need to reach more formal cooperative arrangements among themselves with the object, inter alia, of increasing the range of available and accessible materials. In the United Kingdom, some of the schemes of library cooperation date back to the 1930s, the Sheffield Interchange Organisation (SINTO) being the first. (6) But there has been a steady growth in the number and type of these arrangements since, and in the early 1970s they totalled more than thirty. In 1964 the Standing Conference of Cooperative Library Information Services (SCOCLIS) was formed.

In these schemes there is a considerable emphasis on information, for example in the form of guides to resources and union lists of periodicals. The associated costs are usually borne by the participant libraries, but since they are for the most part labour costs, they do not necessarily show as additional expenditure. Loss of autonomy, if any, is usually small, because the demands made on participant libraries rarely go beyond what they would expect to concede in the customary provision of service. There is very little call for protocols, any agreements usually being of a very simple kind, the libraries' governing bodies in any case retaining their previous authority unimpaired (and with it their right to withdraw from the arrangement). Machinery is also usually of the simplest, implying occasional meetings of staff at appropriate levels to monitor progress of existing arrangements or to explore new possibilities.

Although these arrangements have certainly improved access to published materials in individual localities, they have never been conceived

115

of as an answer to space problems or other economic constraints, and usually not as a positive step towards achieving economies. They are best construed as a more formalised extension of librarians' helpfulness, which has already been remarked upon as the simple foundation of much library cooperation.

Cooperative acquisitions

The schemes described so far seek to maximise the utilisation of stock purchased by libraries in the pursuit of normal acquisitions policies and to maximise the reader's ability to exploit local library resources. Scheme of cooperative acquisition go further, in that they call for some modification of libraries' existing acquisitions policies.

In the UK after the Second World War there was a growth of interest in cooperative acquisitions, as exemplified by the creation of the Metropolitan Special Collections Scheme (7), and later the South-eastern Region Library System (8). These schemes sought to divide responsibility for the acquisition and permanent retention of current British publications between participant libraries. They were inspired by a wish to ensure more comprehensive coverage and availability of the literature. The costs implied were modest, and the loss of autonomy relatively insignificant. Associated machinery was in some cases fairly ambitious, since the Region Library Bureaux usually fulfilled this role. And there were of course protocols; the persistence with which libraries have pursued their allocated specialities to the present day is evidence of how seriously they were taken Information was held in and supplied from a central point and had to be specifically sought.

However, economy of space was not a significant motive and economy of provision was (again) significant only inasmuch as the schemes were seen as methods of maximising the usefulness of expenditure rather than reducing its overall level.

Similar motives can be recognised behind the Background Materials Scheme for older publications and behind such area specialisation scheme as that established by the Standing Conference on Library Materials on Africa (SCOLMA) in 1966. This scheme was reviewed in 1969 and the standing conference's 1977 annual meeting contained news of a further proposed review, suggesting at least that the scheme still merits serious attention. (9)

In these schemes of cooperative acquisition, the information element is often kept to a minimum; frequently, it is defined by the original protocol setting up the scheme. And it is claimed as a virtue of this type of

116

scheme that further information, for example about holdings, is not needed, but is, rather, implied by the details of the original protocol. Nor is any special machinery required since the unique strengths acquired as a result of schemes of this kind can be made available through the general arrangements used by all libraries. The costs of the protocol, in terms of special acquisitions, are usually specifically designed to be kept at a low level. Each library, it is hoped, will regard the expenditure as insignificant, and their readiness to continue participating in such schemes indicates that they probably do. The loss of autonomy is consequently of the least significant kind. There is, above all, no commitment *not* to buy material in specific fields; each library is still left to make up its own mind on that. And the commitment to take up a special field is often one which the library is happy to accept, because it has some interest in that field anyway.

However, if these schemes were to call for programmes of special acquisitions so extensive as to seriously impair the policies previously followed by individual members, consequently affecting the first priority service to their own clientele, it is likely that such commitments would not be readily accepted. This, presumably, is why schemes of this kind have been kept very modest in scope. Anything more ambitious would have most likely been rejected. Libraries would have preferred to seek other methods of gaining access to material for which there is low demand—or would even have told their readers that it was unobtainable.

Union catalogues

Although actual and proposed schemes for inter-library loans can be traced back at least as far as the seventeenth century, it is the last hundred years of increasing professionalism in librarianship which have seen the gradual development of the widespread and highly sophisticated inter-library loans systems which now operate within many countries and also internationally.

Until about fifteen years ago, the most outstanding feature on the landscape of library cooperation in the UK was the service of the National Central Library, and of the Regional Library Bureaux. Vollans's 1951 survey is the best background. (10) The National Central Library, founded in 1930, grew out of the Central Library for Students which originally developed from a library established by the Workers' Educational Association in conjunction with Toynbee Hall for the purpose of supplying books to University Tutorial and WEA classes. The functions of the library were:

a)   to supply on loan to libraries, or in exceptional cases to individuals, books for study which cannot conveniently be obtained in any other wa

b)   to supply such books on loan to groups of adult students

c)   to act as an exchange or clearing house for mutual loans of such bo‹ as between other libraries

d)   to act as a centre of bibliographical information, both for national and international purposes

e)   to facilitate access to books and information about books

f)   to take such other action as may conduce to the above objects.

The origins of the Regional Library Bureaux have been documented by Sewell (11). Despite the declared functions of the National Central Library, the work of all these bodies came to be devoted principally to the preparation and maintenance of union catalogues from which locatie could be supplied to libraries requesting them.

The late 1950s however saw the arrival on the scene of the National Lending Library for Science and Technology. Funded by the Departme of Scientific and Industrial Research, the library's aim was to provide access to scientific periodicals by making them available from its own st‹ to libraries requesting them. It is interesting to note that at the same time the emphasis placed on union catalogues, both by the NCL and by the Regional Library Bureaux was being questioned: 'If the money that had been poured into regional catalogues and the NCL over the last thir‹ years had been devoted to creating a real National Central Library . . . not a catalogue agency, we should now have a book collection that wou] save most of the passing of forms.' (12) The NCL itself was already expanding its own acquisitions activities in order to be able to lend from stock, rather than provide locations for, such frequently requested (and also in holding libraries, frequently used) materials as American academi press books, and learned publications in some of the more widely read foreign languages.

The subsequent amalgamation in 1973 of the NLLST and the NCL to form the British Library Lending Division is now history. Libraries are still requested to contribute catalogue entries for certain types of ma terials to the BLLD's union catalogues, namely pre-1972 English languaç monographs and foreign monographs of all publication dates. (And it must also be mentioned that an updated regional system, depending on the use of ISSN listings, continues to perform an important function.) However, the most recent study shows that while 83 per cent of valid requests were satisfied by BLLD from stock, only 10 per cent were referred to other UK libraries. (13)

118

The progress of the BLLD has therefore fitted in well with the tendency of libraries to show only lukewarm enthusiasm for systems requiring protocols, machinery, and loss of autonomy, and to prefer one based principally on cost and (less warmly, perhaps) on the input of information to a central place for subsequent output only on specific request. It has also brought two other considerations to the forefront of the discussion of the supply of less used materials, namely speed and simplicity. The BLLD can often provide a quicker service because the provision of that service is the library's first priority, whereas for most libraries it is a priority which ought properly to be placed second after the needs of the library's registered readers. It is significant in this regard that BLLD asks libraries which agree to enter into a special support relationship with them ('back-up' libraries) to be prepared to 'give priority' to requests from BLLD. The simplicity arises from the fact that libraries can now refer all inter-library loan requests to BLLD rather than spend some time trying to determine whence they may best be referred. Though this simplicity is far from being universally used, there is no doubt that for many libraries it has already become a powerful factor deterring them from examining other ways of accessing little-used stock.

It might be expected that the BLLD's policies would have an impact on the policies of individual libraries. This is a point which has been specifically denied recently by Line and Wood (14), though others refuse to concede the case. (15) It would be interesting to see comparative statistics of the growth of the NLLST/BLLD collection, the growth in serials holdings of some of the major United Kingdom learned libraries, and the estimated total world output of serials. This might offer some evidence as to the impact (or lack of it) of these policies. Until such evidence is available, it can at least be argued that this form of 'library co-operation'—and it can be so called principally because it grew partly from the activities of the old NCL and also because union catalogues still feature in its work—has had no impact on libraries' wish or need to achieve steady-state.

A recent postscript on this point arises from the Atkinson Report. Addressing itself to the problems posed by the continuing growth of academic libraries and the building needs thereby implied, it recommended inter alia as follows:

i)   The assessment of future university library building requirements on site should be based on the concept of a self-renewing library, that is, a library of limited size in which beyond a certain point material should be reduced at a rate related to the rate of acquisition.

ii) Once a university's reserve store is filled, it should be expected to dispose of surplus stock, normally to BLLD. (16)

Libraries' preference for a cost-based service, remarked on above, is here pushed even further. The library's own mounting storage costs are to be curbed, and in the steady-state equation the only elements suscept of growth are to be the costs of using the inter-library loans system, and the costs of stock relegation. The extent to which libraries may be likely to experience growth in these costs is not quantified in the report.

In one sense, therefore, there has been a progression in library 'co-operation' which has culminated in a greatly increased reliance on BLLD Many libraries now regard the BLLD services as the only supplement to their own stock which is available or needed. The value and potential of current schemes of cooperation need to be measured, it can be argued, by setting their costs and attractiveness against those of the BLLD servic

Nonetheless, there is a persistent thread of argument which considers the BLLD services to be no replacement for the traditional forms of co-operation. Guttsman is one of the advocates of this view. (17) Is the Bl the sole and permanent remedy for libraries' own deficiencies of stock? Is it a temporary remedy, very effective in the present time scale, but a product of a particular stage in the development of communications, inf mation handling, and even political ideology (the central government as universal provider), to be phased out or reduced in importance in its tur as times change? Are the BLLD and other cooperative arrangements mutually complementary, though their respective functions may alter from time to time? The answer to these questions depends in some measure on the present achievements and on the potential future of libr cooperation.

Library cooperation re-assessed

It is well to summarise here two important considerations derived fro the retrospective survey of library cooperation. The first is that 'these efforts have usually taken the form of relatively low-priority, individual programs grafted onto an existing organisational structure, doing little to alter basic operations or perceptions of service, and lacking the qualit of inter-related program objectives.' (18) As the president of the US Re-search Libraries Group (comprising Yale, Harvard, Columbia and New York Public Libraries) goes on to say: 'The distinctive characteristic of RLG was the commitment to improve services and reduce the rate of increase in operating costs by restructuring the fundamental policies, procedures and service objectives of member libraries.' This can be take

120

as an acid test of a cooperative scheme. Provided that participation does not affect the procedures of the library in the most fundamental respects, libraries have usually been willing or even enthusiastic participants. However, such arrangements are really a means of demonstrating that spirit of helpfulness towards colleagues summarised earlier in the quotation by Davey. And alongside it there still remains the spirit of self-sufficiency.

The other point to make is that very few cooperative activities have been promoted by consideration of the need to save space. If libraries are able to refer readers elsewhere for some of their needs, then one of the implications is that space is saved in the library of first resort since books and periodicals for which accommodation would otherwise have been required is not needed. If libraries enter into cooperative acquisitions programmes with one another, this also implies that less space is required in each of the individual libraries to accommodate their share of the total material than if they had each bought it all. Yet in most of the British cooperative activities which I have described, space considerations are given no weight at all, and in the few in which they are referred to, they are considered to be of very low importance. Recent American evidence, however, shows some small signs of an increasing awareness of the need to save space, yet there too, the space problem is not seen as imperative. A brief aside on the issue of the economics of space is called for.

In their *Economics of academic libraries* (19), Baumol and Marcus offer us:

what we believe to be as complete and thorough an analysis as possible of the available economic data on college and university libraries . . . We have constructed a set of analytic interrelationships which permit us to derive statistical estimates of the interrelations of some of the most critical economic variables relating to library operations . . . The results of our analysis . . . can be used by individual librarians in making plans for their own institutions, by college and university administrators in anticipating the future fiscal needs of their libraries and evaluating the financial consequences of decisions on overall institutional policy and by organisations representing librarians in making their case for the resources they need and determining lines of research that will be most useful in planning for the future.

In chapter two of the book, there is an attempt 'to identify the factors which determine library costs and to estimate the magnitude of their effects.' Staff and acquisitions costs were examined and were found to account for almost 90 per cent of library operating costs. Binding, equipment, inter-library loan costs and other operating expenditures

121

were taken into account. Space costs however appear to have been excluded from operating costs.

I have suggested earlier in this chapter the possible reasons why such a approach is used—and also why it ought not to be. However, once the economics of space are brought into the discussion, the argument becom very dense. It has already been pointed out that space costs and other costs are interrelated; restrictions on space imply costs in relegation and/ reductions in acquisitions programmes, and increased inter-library loans. For the user they imply added costs of travel to other collections, the cost of time lost in waiting for and sometimes never receiving material ordered on inter-library loan, and also a lost opportunity cost. This arise because it can clearly be argued that certain material will never be consulted at all by the user if it is not actually on the shelves of his own libr

This need not necessarily be due to indolence. Available bibliographi resources may not indicate the existence of the item or may omit to sho its relevance to the topic in question. This of course is the reverse side o the positive argument in favour of browsing, and, as with browsing, there is a lack of any hard evidence as to its importance other than the repeate insistence of many people who ought to know—which, in the absence of other evidence, ought not to be disregarded. Economists however would take the argument much further. In addition to the depreciation costs o a library, some would wish to take into consideration the imputed cost also, that is they would wish to calculate the income an institution woul have obtained by investing the money expended on library services, and, after deducting the economic benefits conferred by the library (and how are they to be calculated?) they would regard the balance of lost income as part of the cost of the service. (If acquisitions costs are really a form capital costs, they too ought to be considered to have imputed costs.) T is the stage at which the non-economist regretfully concludes that one d of the argument is so far not completely within his grasp.

Yet enough has been said, by Baumol and Marcus, and by critics of th Atkinson Report, to suggest that capital costs may not be such a signific element as is often supposed in the financial commitment implied by a large library. In the UK, steady-state has been assumed to imply a restri tion on growth regardless of its repercussive effects. What is needed is a formula which correctly relates building costs to other costs of library provision, indeed to all aspects of the provision and use of information.

The new imperatives

In the USA, the growth in cooperative arrangements (consortia and resource sharing are the currently preferred terms of art) has been truly spectacular in recent years. A large directory of such consortia has recently been published and includes over four hundred consortia. (20) This rapid growth is a phenomenon which clearly requires attention. In a paper entitled 'Progress towards goals in library resource sharing' at the 1976 Pittsburgh Conference on Resource Sharing in Libraries, Galvin and Murphy identified 'four distinct, but closely interrelated "imperatives" ' which they considered lay at the heart of this development, namely the philosophical, the fiscal, the empirical, and the technological. The first of these is concerned with the growth of recorded knowledge, rising user expectations, greater orientation towards user satisfaction by libraries and rising standards laid down by appropriate bodies. The second is concerned with libraries' increasing financial problems and the stern examination of priorities this inspires. The third concerns the impact of research into book use and readers' habits which has tended to erode librarians' self confidence in collection building. The fourth is identified primarily with computer technology, but reprographic and other technologies are not to be entirely discounted. The four are seen as together creating a transformation in the climate for the development of cooperation between libraries. It is interesting to consider them in the light of the principal considerations about library cooperation previously outlined.

A pattern for the future

I now propose to present some features of a possible form of cooperative arrangement between libraries which might take fullest account of this changed climate. It is derived in some measure from experience and discussions at the University of London, but is not totally limited to that. Other details, and amplifications, have been included, and any comments I make should not be construed as being critical of the University of London—which itself has its own particular legacy to cope with. It is in fact an attempt to describe a system in which information is a by-product of essential, internal library procedures; protocols and machinery are designed for those areas in which they are more likely to be cost-effective; loss of autonomy is substantial; costs are significant, but, it is hoped, reasonable in proportion to the benefits. And libraries together retain the sense of controlling their own destiny. It also takes account of the imperatives referred to by Galvin and Murphy.

The first point to make is that the libraries concerned must be reasonably closely situated to one another. It was pointed out earlier that sending the reader to the book is often the alternative to bringing the book to the reader. If that costs a lot in time and transport expenses, then it becomes less attractive as an option and a heavier premium is placed on inter-library loans. Therefore, the further apart the libraries are, the less justification there is for cooperation and the greater the reason to prefer a direct, BLLD-type lending service. And the residual problem remains of materials which cannot be called up by inter-library loan either becaus there is no adequate bibliographical reference to them or because inter-library loan is an inappropriate way of bringing them into use.

The most obvious area of potential cooperation is periodical holdings. The holdings of cooperating libraries would need to be recorded in a uni catalogue, but one in which the data which was input was necessary for the library's own record of its holdings. The production of the union lis would therefore be almost a by-product of the individual library lists. N subscriptions to periodicals would be taken out after consultation betwe the libraries as to which member of the consortium ought to subscribe. There may, of course, be thought to be a need for more than one subscri tion. Some periodicals holdings would be recognised as unique consortiu sets, and holding libraries would have a special commitment to retain the Others could be cancellable, after a further due process of consultation i financial circumstances (or the falling quality of the contents) appeared to make this desirable. A distinction could be made between initial use periodicals and continuing use. Most periodicals get heavy use in the firs year or two after publication, by scholars keeping up with their field. After that, use declines. Therefore there may be a need for more than o subscription but for only one set to be bound and retained. Subject to satisfactory arrangements, there would be scope for economies in storag and binding. And on the matter of storage the availability of journals from BLLD could be a significant consideration.

Cooperation in respect of monographs would be less rewarding becau the cost of the machinery would be greater and the potential savings usu smaller and limited to a single occasion. Nonetheless a common, prefera on-line, union catalogue of current mongraphs designed to include infor-mation about potential requirements and materials on order would give libraries an effortless awareness of the acquisitions activities of other li-braries, and enable them to develop their policies in detail accordingly. The savings would be particularly significant on the more expensive indi vidual items where a full process of consultaion between interested libra could be cost effective. The catalogue could, arguably, at some stage be limited to material of that kind. It would also be possible to carry forwa the integration of monograph stock into a relegation and retention polic

Integration from the user's point of view would also be needed. The would have to be ready access for the user of any one of the libraries to all the other libraries in the consortium, and a document delivery system which was sufficient for those instances where an inter-library loan of the original or of a copy was the most appropriate means of bringing the user and the material together.

The system here described in summary would need to be worked out in many small details. However, its essential features are clear. Between the libraries of the consortium, there would be a very substantial inter-availability of information, about stock, about readers, about acquisitions, retention and relegation policies, but much of the information supplied would be available as an incidental to each library's internal processes. This would tend to reduce and/or conceal the true costs of running the consortium. There would be extensive machinery, and the protocols required would also be far reaching. The implications for library autonomy would be substantial. It is therefore clear that the system described, the system made possible by and indicated by Galvin and Murphy's four imperatives is one which runs counter to the pattern of behaviour instinctively followed by libraries in the past in cooperative activities. If it is to have good prospects of success, this can only be because libraries have concluded that the pattern of constraints has changed so sharply that a totally new pattern of library provision must emerge.

And they must also decide that this pattern is the right one. At present there is discussion of the economies of BLLD provision and those of compact local or remote store of less used materials. Some work has been done on this in the specific London setting. (21) It shows that a remote store is more expensive in providing what it does provide than use of BLLD would be. However, BLLD's charges are known to be insufficient to recover the whole cost of running the division. If total BLLD costs are taken into account, remote store proves in this case to be cheaper. But considerations of speed and simplicity also need taking into account.

This is not strictly a case of choosing the better of two alternatives. Libraries of all types may look to the BLLD to provide materials they themselves have decided to relegate. They may also look to it for those marginal requirements which it would have seemed inappropriate to purchase even had the BLLD not existed. The choice is therefore in the first instance between a two-fold pattern of provision (on-site plus BLLD) or a three-fold pattern (on-site, plus remote store, plus BLLD). Only a consortium which had the ambition to achieve among its several participants a level of acquisitions equal to that of BLLD could claim to have made a straight choice between two alternative and mutually exclusive modes of provision. Even in that case, BLLD's realisation that in respect of some

125

materials it may be preferable to rely on other libraries (in certain cases, specifically designated as 'back-up' libraries) is an indication that self-sufficiency is unlikely ever to be achieved even by the most powerful grouping. A typical case is that of material from certain Third World countries. Supply of these materials can often depend on good personal contacts. The amount of material under discussion is small, though for some library users it may represent a very high proportion of demand.

Libraries inevitably expect to provide the most heavily used materials from their own resources. The argument about the effectiveness of consortia, and the effectiveness of BLLD itself is about providing access to little used materials.

Some aspects of this argument are of general application. They are concerned for example with questions of reader behaviour, with the economics of opportunities for consultation provided or denied, with the characteristics of the primary literature or the secondary bibliographical resources in some subject fields. Yet every act of library use takes place in a specific situation and many aspects of the argument must of necessity be specially applicable to that context, that place and that time only. Research is greatly needed on aspects of access to less used materials. If the research can make progress towards the establishment of a general equation which will help librarians to appreciate the balance of benefits between local provision consortium creation (to what pattern?) and participation, and reliance on outside resources, then libraries may be better able to choose rationally between policy options and be less driven to choose more by instinct or prejudice and to have to defend their choice in those terms against the contrary instinct and prejudices of others.

Summary

Libraries have traditionally made, or used, cooperative arrangements only to satisfy a very small residual proportion of the total demand they experience. They have felt no obligation to expand their services to meet all this residual demand, nor have they been prepared to incur the loss of autonomy implied by more far reaching cooperative arrangements. The implications of these arrangements for space provision and other aspects of library expenditure have been negligible. Meanwhile a centralised service has grown up which may meet all of this residual demand for the foreseeable future and certainly meets a high proportion of it at the present time. Varuous factors are currently placing pressure on libraries to enter into more thoroughgoing cooperative arrangements. Whether these arrangements will achieve the desired effects is as yet unproven. B

126

it will need a very great change in libraries' present attitudes towards co-operation, if this is to have a substantial impact on libraries' current financial and space problems. And all the while the BLLD services remain to be reckoned with. Experimentation and research are both needed, and open minds to weigh the results for the best advantage of libraries.

REFERENCES

1 J Cohen 'Book cost and book use: the economics of a university library' Paper prepared for the Pittsburgh Conference on Resource Sharing in Libraries, September 29-October 1, 1976.

2 W Ashworth 'Self-renewing libraries' *New library world* 78 (921), March 1977, 47-48.

3 The important leader in this area of investigation is R W Trueswell who has published more than one article on this theme. His work on book use has had many followers, who have carried its implications into various aspects of library administration.

4 For example C Harris 'A comparison of issues and in-library use of books' *Aslib proceedings* 29 (3), March 1977, 118-126.

5 J S Davey 'Library cooperation' *British librarianship and information science 1966-1970* Ed H A Whatley. London, Library Association, 1972.

6 J P Lamb 'The organisation for the interchange of technical publications in Sheffield and district' *Serial slants* 6 (1), 1955, 6-14.

7 D Leggatt 'The metropolitan special collections scheme' *Library Association record* 51 (6), 1949, 186.

8 W J L Hill 'Subject specialisation in the south-eastern region' *Library Association record* 52 (7), 1950, 229-230.

9 *Conference on the acquisition of material from Africa . . . 1969 Reports and papers* Comp Valerie Bloomfield. Zug, Inter-Documentation Co, 1969.

10 R F Vollans *Library cooperation in Great Britain: report of a survey of the National Central Library and the Regional Bureaux* London, National Central Library, 1952, xii, 139.

11 P H Sewell *The regional library systems* 2nd ed. London, Library Association 1956, 71.

12 F M Gardner 'Prospects and policies' *Librarian* 48 (3) 1959, 49-53.

13 *BLL review* 4 (4), October 1976, 112-113.

14 M B Line and D N Wood 'The effect of a large-scale photocopying service on journal sales' *Journal of documentation* 31 (4), 1975, 234-245.

15 E van Tongeren 'The effect of a large-scale photocopying service on journal sales' *Journal of documentation* 32 (3), Sept 1976, 198-204. See also the reply by Line and Wood, 204-206.

16 University Grants Committee *Capital provision for university libraries: report of a working party* London, HMSO, 1976, 40.

17 W L Guttsman 'Why a national library system should be a network not a pyramid' *Times higher education supplement* 6 August 1976, 11.

18 Research Libraries Group (J E Skipper, President). *Annual report 1975-1976* Branford, Conn, 1976, 2.

19 W J Baumol and M Marcus *Economics of academic libraries* Washington, American Council on Education, 1973. xii, 98.

20 D V Black and C A Cuadra *Directory of academic library consort.* Santa Monica, Calif, Systems Development Corporation, 1975.

21 University of London Interim Library Resources Coordinating Committee *Report on the depository library* London, 1975, 18.

STEADY-STATE AND NATIONAL LIBRARIES

Stephen Green

If truth is not to be found on the shelves of the British Museum, where . . . is truth?—Virginia Woolf, 1929

THE KEYSTONE of a country's library system is the national library, whether it be recognised formally as such in legislation or informally in the central service functions attributed to it. Its central position can be conceived as either an innovative or a responsive one, and in practice it is often a synthesis of the two. A significant change in the style and scope of operation of any particular segment of the system can produce repercussions in the type of services offered by the national library; and of course the converse is also true.

The recent espousal of the doctrine of 'steady-state' by those responsible for funding university and research libraries may be construed as an example of such an interaction. The merits and demerits of the doctrine have been propounded and analysed extensively in the professional literature of the United Kingdom, the United States, Australia and other similar countries where the economic, social and historical profile allows the philosophy of 'zero-growth' to have its advocates. Whilst other chapters in this book explore these arguments in some detail, my own concern is to speculate on the positive consequences of the doctrine for a national library. I shall argue that its adoption raises both direct and indirect questions for the future of the national collections. Directly, it can increase the importance of the central loan collection, if a country has one, and pose new challenges for its management. However, since this has already been considered in the literature (1), I shall pay equal attention to the questions that indirectly may be provoked about the national reference collections which, broadly speaking, constitute the nation's major archive of domestic and foreign printed material. In this respect the essay's scope ranges considerably wider than the issues of the contemporary steady-state debate.

I make no apologies for dealing in generalities, anathema as they are to many librarians. Nevertheless I will draw inevitably on my experience and

129

observations of 'the country I know best', to borrow the euphemism practised by nationals serving in the European Commission. *Mutatis mutandis*, extrapolation should be possible for other national environments.

The two phrases national library and steady-state present problems of terminology which should be treated briefly. First, it has to be recognised that the phrase (or sometimes only the concept, lacking the explicit title) 'national library' is an omnibus one, embodying a heterogeneity of functions, responsibilities and organisational forms. Some national libraries derive from the ancient royal, court or personal collections, others are linked closely to the growth of political systems like the democratic legislatures which have flourished from the nineteenth century onwards, or the twentieth century socialist state. Yet others—particularly in the Third World—are very recent creations where the emphasis on national bibliographical services may be greater proportionally than that on collection, preservation and the amplification of a long and deep cultural past which has been manifested in its documents. In each case, the formal and actual relationship with the other components in the national library and information system is unique in character. It is therefore inevitable that the response of each library to the steady-state doctrine will differ, at least in some details.

Secondly, whilst it is true that the reaction of many university libraries in 1976 and 1977 has echoed that of the medieval virgin and martyr St Wiborada whose cry when her abbey was being attacked by the barbarians was 'Save the books first! Hide them!', other sectors of the library community have long practised stock-renewal policies. Even the largest public library systems weed their stock regularly (2), and the specialist libraries serving the needs of industry and commerce have built up a deliberate reliance on the central loan stock wherever possible; in the United Kingdom this dependence on the British Library Lending Division is positively endorsed by large companies like ICI as a cost-effective means of supporting research without diminishing its quality or timeliness. The steady-state doctrine has ranged wider in its application than just university and research libraries. Nevertheless it is precisely the nature and needs of the advanced user of university collections that has stimulated much of the current debate; a user who, it is claimed, is a very different animal from the public or special library client.

In many countries the relationship between the national library and university libraries is symbiotic but not hierarchical. This is certainly true in the UK. The closeness of purpose is expressed through the British Library's extensive involvement in the affairs of the Standing Conference

130

of National and University Librarians; through members of the university community—both librarians and academics—serving on the British Library's Advisory Council and Committees (about 27 per cent of the total membership), and on the more informal meetings structured to discuss particular issues and areas of interest; through the universities' frequent calls on the library's lending collections and through the participation of some of the major university collections in the Lending Division's back-up arrangements. There has always been a close accord between those libraries with collections of great national importance (the School of Oriental and African Studies and the Institute of Advanced Legal Studies are two examples) and both the Lending and Reference Divisions of the British Library, if only because their user typologies are so akin. In the area of research and development sponsored by the British Library, many projects are located within universities and their libraries and two research centres—for user studies and for research into primary communications respectively—have been established recently at the universities of Sheffield and Leicester. Perhaps the most striking indication of the traditional university—national library nexus is the fact that there is probably a greater interchange of professional and scholarly staff between the British Library (especially the Reference Division), and the universities than between the British Library and any other sector of the library community.

Such a relationship cannot be static, and the advent of the steady-state library is an opportunity for it to develop, if the librarians so wish. In the UK some librarians are hesitant about what they believe to be an over-reliance on central acquisition and storage facilities, although they should be mindful that many of the arguments now being rehearsed with infant vigour are not new. In the United States the need to limit the heady growth of university library stock was proposed as early as 1899 by Charles V Eliot, the President of Harvard University, in his annual report. He initiated a debate of some years' duration. (3) Then in 1949 Ernest Colwell, the President of the University of Chicago, published a paper in which he wrote 'Libraries resemble cemeteries in the fact that much of what they contain is good for nothing except to enrich the soil. If 50 per cent of what college and university libraries contain was spread on the fields, it would enrich education as well as the soil'. (4) He wanted a 'fixed ceiling research library', backed up by 'a regional library—a librarian's library'. His powerful beliefs led to the Midwest Inter-library Center in 1951, renamed in 1965 the Center for Research Libraries, with a national remit. In the UK, the conditions favourable to the advancement of the steady-state doctrine were created with a more unconscious stealth, through the establishment of what became the National Central Library in 1916, the National Lending Library for Science and Technology in 1961, and the their amalgamation into the British Library Lending Division in 1973. However the prescriptions of the University Grants Committee Working Party on Capital Provision for Libraries did not depend upon these developments in a fundamental sense, although undoubtedly facilitated by them. For the UGC it was primarily the fact that its limited capital resources were being outstripped by the demands of universities in the post-Robbins era. Its tiered solution may be reprehensible or distastefu or ill-researched, but it is not possessed of striking originality.

The utilisation of the services of the Lending Division of the British Library as the ultimate store of the nation's least-used research material suggested itself without difficulty to the UGC working party. The divis reputation has been built on the features of supply, which is speedy and cheap in comparison with other forms of inter-library loan; of high-den storage in a part of the country where accommodation costs are relative low; and of an acquisitions policy devoted to acquiring all significant periodicals (irrespective of language) and all English language monograp for which a demand can be envisaged. Its style of stock management h owed at least as much to warehouse as to classical library techniques although the style, which was evolved originally to cater for a predominantly scientific and technical serial literature collection, has undergon some modification with the expansion of its remit to cover all disciplin including those more heavily dependent on information and interpretat contained in monographs. The proposals of the working party may als be seen as no more than an extension of present practice, since the Len Division already receives a substantial number of donations. In a samp taken between July 1974 and December 1975, universities represented 11 per cent of the donors, but 34 per cent of the total donations, more than any other type of library. (5) Allardyce and Line estimate that if the UGC's proposals were implemented in full, the annual rate of dona might increase four-fold eventually. This is a very substantial increase, posing financial and administrative problems, but not one which from Lending Division's point of view is likely to initiate bibliographic revol amongst the existing procedures on which its reputation, and therefore its appeal to the working party, are based.

However the questions must not be represented as those only about technical capability, but also as ones about desirability, which in turn a founded on assumptions or evidence about the nature of scholarship ar research and the relative costs of local versus central storage. These ha been considered earlier in the book, but it is worth emphasising that they must be answered by the universities and the UGC themselves, however helpful the British Library is in supplying data about the costs, speed and reliability of its own services. It is also fair to say that the British Library could not entertain the additional burden which the proposals imply without a corresponding recognition of it by central government in its financing.

A legitimate question mark does hang over the possibility of more restrictive legislation concerning library reprography in the wake of the Whitford Committee Report (6), since the proportion of requests satisfied by photography from the Lending Division has grown from 24 per cent in 1969 to 80 per cent in 1976. Such legislation would increase the costs and diminish the speed of the existing service, but in all probability these adverse consequences would fall less heavily upon the type of material which might be sent to the Lending Division according to the working party's proposals than on other types because it would be less likely to be in copyright.

One of the main points of contention at the Loughborough seminar on the future of library collections was the necessity or otherwise for browsing, especially in the humanities. The term, in common with its highbrow twin serendipity, does indeed represent what purports to be a legitimate research method in some disciplines but in the current debate it has been used too loosely, to the detriment of rational argument. It carries the nuance of purposeless, frivolous leisure splendidly evoked in P G Wodehouse's phrase 'excellent browsing and sluicing'. In fact browsing has a number of very different manifestations. At one level it does entail wandering optimistically—often as an antidote to temporary boredom—to a section of the classified stock on open-access and selecting items at random, as some critics of the process would have us believe. However a much more prevalent and serious form is following a reference at a timely point in one's research with reasonable hope that one will find the item referred to in the local stock fairly quickly. At this level the impetus to browse will be inhibited severely if the local stock is so slim that it is likely that any slightly obscure reference will have to be supplied through an inter-library loan service which at best demands a wait of some days before delivery, especially if one is aware that a financial contribution or a special justification to the parsimonious library staff may be required from the user. Furthermore, with substantial research collections to hand one may in the course of a day chase a chain of references, each dependent on the step (ie the item) before. Reliance on external services to achieve

133

the same result must mean a wait at least equivalent to the minimum period of delivery multiplied by the number of steps in chain, even discounting a failure of human stamina or interest.

To suggest that the browsing technique can be superseded by loading library shelves with more bibliographies, abstracts and indexes is in my view a glib and spurious solution. Whilst it cannot be denied that 'many libraries have woefully inadequate collections of abstracting and indexing journals' and that universities should not only improve their stocks but also encourage a more comprehensive coverage of the literature than exists at present, this is an argument to support the browsing technique rather than an increased reliance on a central bookstore. (7, 8) After all, a reference or a lead may be found in these worthy bibliographical tools just as much as in a footnote or a library catalogue: they are all sources with a speculative value. Faced with a reference (or more likely, a number of them), the crucial distinction for the research library user concerns the geographical location of the actual item and the time needed to get it. It will be a long time, if ever, before the identification of an entry in the bibliographical tools which may serve the user of the older literature in the humanities and some of the social sciences will carry with it a guarantee of automatic and rapid availability. If the validity of browsing is to be vitiated by the triumph of specious reasoning, the possibility of making new connections between different disciplinary fields, techniques and ideas—not necessarily catered for in the coverage and division between different bibliographical publications prevailing at the time—will be hampered irreparably with profound results for the future of scholarship

Before leaving the question of the utility and the inherent limitations of separating the activity of research (particularly that with an historical content) from the location of its raw materials, there is perhaps a cautionary tale in the German research library experience as described by the historian Johannes Haller in his memoirs. (9) From the turn of the century, the increasing volume of research material had been outstripping the funds made available by the German states to libraries except in the case of Berlin. A sophisticated network of interlibrary loan between and within the states was begun. The result according to Haller was that library budgets stayed at their long since inadequate levels, requests for new acquisitions being refused on the grounds that everything could be got from Berlin; foreign literature especially was acquired in quite inadequate quantities, and the demands on Berlin grew heavier and heavier, with a consequent growing delay in supply. In Haller's view 'at the very period of Germany's central role in world politics, German scholarship ceased to concern itself with what was being printed in the rest of the world', with disastrous results. However in fairness it should be noted that no special provision could be made for a comprehensive central loan stock which certainly must have aggravated the frustrations of the users.

In so far as the adoption of the steady-state doctrine in the 1970s will have the effect of reducing the local availability of research material (beyond the salutary weeding out of truly and permanently dead stock (10)), it may throw an unexpected spotlight upon the nature and use of the national library's reference collections, which are wholly or mainly non-loanable. This indirect effect has been barely noticed in the debate so far. Yet if the capabilities for serious browsing as defined above are significantly reduced in many university libraries and if it is something more than an indulgent habit, then it is reasonable to suppose that the erstwhile users of these libraries will turn increasingly to the national reference collections. This will be particularly true in the UK if the really outstanding university collections in special fields, which at present share some of the pressure put upon the British Library Reference Division, are not sufficiently exempt from the general application of the doctrine.

One obvious objection to this hypothesis is that although the Reference Division contains a universe of source material its stock is almost entirely on closed access unlike most university libraries and even in the proposed new premises at Somers Town the open access provision is envisaged at no more than 4 per cent of the total (although rising from the present 0.4 per cent). It is true that retrieval of an item is slower than in an open access library but it is a situation which compares favourably with retrieval through the inter-library loan network. In any case the merits of open access in a library beyond a certain size are not unqualified, as a leading disputant in the steady-state controversy argued some years ago. (11) Most importantly it does still permit, I would contend, the most important form of browsing in a modified form, with the call-slip replacing the walk from the catalogue to the shelves. In an environment which in practice closely simulates the conditions in a major university library—as evidenced by the easy movement of scholars between the two—the fact of closed access is an objection which cannot be satisfactorily sustained.

This augmented role for the national library's reference collections could evolve without any conscious decisions by its managers. Yet this is unlikely partly because there may well be growing external pressures and developing expectations for the library to articulate its policies for acquisition, preservation and exploitation. Looked at in another light, one consequence for the national library's reference service could be a fortuitous opportunity to place itself more firmly within the structure of the national system than ever before. Thus it is appropriate that my remaining reflections should be on the nature and future of the national reference collections. Although I have only questions and propositions to pu which could form an agenda for further consideration, it is not a premat exercise. All great reference collections achieve change slowly, not unlik the stately ocean liner which is reputed to take twelve miles to slow dow and two hours to go through a ninety degrees turn. The agenda of quest will not be exhaustive—that might be too intimidating—but it will allow rudimentary examination to be made of some main areas of concern, wh are a definition of the collections, their permanence, their comprehensiv ness now and in the future, and possible developments in their exploitati

I must emphasise that these personal animadversions do not represent a collective British Library view in any way, either in what I have said so far or what now follows.

The national reference collections consist of two distinct components to their custodians and managers at least. First, there is what may be termed the national archive of the printed word and image. This has bee built up through gift, bequest, purchase and above all through the provisions of legal deposit which most national libraries enjoy. Secondly th are the research collections of foreign literature: for the British Library, this is reckoned for current acquisitions to be between 5 per cent and 8 per cent of the total published output according to area. In recent years the national printed archive has come to a new prominence as the principles and programmes of universal bibliographical control (UBC) and universal availability of publications (UAP) have been enunciated and implemented. However, beware of the primrose path of subscribing too enthusiastically to the new dogma that each country should be held primarily responsible for collecting, recording and making available materia published within its own boundaries, since it may lead in this imperfect world of tumult, war, destruction and political caprice to an over-relianc on others. It resembles on an international scale the steady-state logic ir the sense that supply from a remote location is preferred to local acquisition. There is also a further note of warning to be sounded for the ma national collections of foreign literature if they are viewed as an entity which can be developed without taking into account the resources whic already exist elsewhere within the country. Obviously the position of t national library is unique but it does not follow necessarily that it shoul stand aloof from cooperative acquisition schemes or refuse to offer supp to other centres of excellence where its remit allows. Instead it should try to determine more explicitly its special position within the national system, and to establish to what extent it is in the interests of users to encourage different collocations of overlapping material in a variety of locations, given that resources are finite. These are questions on which there are views, but very little sustained research and thought so far has taken place.

The national reference collections have been regarded traditionally as a permanent record, immune from the stock discarding virus. Their defenders claim that this is imperative for a number of reasons. First, the collections are an indispensable artefact of a nation's cultural heritage, like national galleries and museums. To maintain them is an act of cultural faith. Secondly, they represent the most comprehensive record of indigenous publishing and as such constitute a unique archive. Thirdly, the cost of maintaining them is nugatory in comparison with other uses to which public money is put. Fourthly, the collections in themselves provide evidence of a nation's intellectual history, showing the emphasis and shifts of scholarly concerns through what has been selected over the years. Finally (though there may be other mainstream arguments I have neglected inadvertently), even if it is accepted that the collections contain some detritus it is impossible to devise criteria for retention or rejection which can take into account the always unpredictable fashions of scholarship and use: today's trivia is tomorrow's research evidence.

Whilst having fundamental emotional sympathy with these propositions I am disturbed by the intuitive and peremptory way in which they are usually advanced. Is not a more rigorous justification required as a matter of urgency? Unless the research community—users and librarians alike—can buttress the philosophy of permanent retention in a more detailed and sophisticated manner, in a way that will stand up to external scrutiny by those who have many competing claims on their time and purse, it may be ill-prepared to refute successfully the challenge when and if it comes. By its very nature the rationale cannot be developed quickly.

What sorts of challenges might the advocate of change put forward? It might be argued that the cost of acquiring and maintaining the requisite storage space, often on prime metropolitan sites, is disproportionate in relation to the useful value of the stock thus housed. The critic will point forcefully to the continuing growth in the volume of literature published annually and needing to be housed, summoning-up an image in the mind of the lay public of the inner city being swamped by a rising tide of rubbish and superseded knowledge. Vivid statistics of the 'information

137

explosion' come easily to hand, such as the estimate that the current
bibliographies in science are equivalent in volume to the total output of
scientific literature a century ago. Then it might be argued that a distinc
tion should be made between literature of permanent value and that whi
has a limited lifespan, the latter to be disposed of after a certain period.
(Be warned: this particular critic will need strong evidence that the paris
magazine, the local telephone directory or the fourth edition of a popula
textbook will be not only liable to use in the future, but also of value to
the commonweal. His breed is not at all convinced that the PhD industr
is intrinsically wholesome.) Perhaps a more subtle challenge is presented
the critic who accepts the validity of aiming at a total national archive, b
presses the case for weeding the foreign collections, which are not part
of the national heritage in the same sense. Surely the selectors of oversea
material do make mistakes of judgement on occasion, which can be reco
nised with hindsight?

So far it has been assumed that within national reference collections
the national printed archive is completely comprehensive. It has not bee
it is not, and it is likely to be less so in future. I will comment on the U
situation, though it is probably applicable to other countries. The Britis
Museum's right to receive free of charge a copy of every item published
in this country was never fully exercised, even after the 1911 Copyright
Act. In 1932 certain categories of material—trade advertisements, local
transport timetables, calendars, blank forms and wall sheets—were specif
cally exempted. In practice there was a much broader passive exclusions
policy whereby further categories of items were not pursued if publisher
chose not to deposit. These included the now more traditional forms of
non-book material (for example, posters or microfilm), non-commerciall
published theses, correspondence courses, unnumbered research reports,
programmes of public events, promotional literature, many local government publications, commercial exhibition catalogues and annual reports
of bodies not publicly accountable. It was in effect the judicious exercis
of a kind of quality control, and it continues in many respects today. It
is no coincidence that much of this material is difficult to process, store
and retrieve.

However, today and for the future the problem of comprehensiveness
assumes a new dimension because of three essential changes in the forma
of communication. These are the burgeoning of cheap reprographic
facilities, the increasing use of microform as a means of original publication and the possibilities inherent in computer-based electronic communications.

The copying machine and low-cost offset technology have created opportunities for people to 'publish' (a notoriously difficult word to define with any precision) which did not exist before. Whereas a member of a 1920s unestablished and unregarded writers' cooperative would have been content to circulate at most a few manuscript copies of his latest work around his particular coterie, his counterpart today is inclined to distribute his work much more widely at low cost, perhaps placing an invitation to acquire in a classified advertisement in a literary journal. This constitutes publication, but more often than not the author will not be aware of the obligation to deposit, and the national library will be fortunate to learn of its existence. Likewise the stream, or rather the torrent, of radical underground literature of the 1960s and 1970s has been largely neglected by the national library, although some university libraries have been able to make greater efforts.

Yet it is not a problem confined to what some would regard as the esoteric fringes of society, for Her Majesty's Government is one of the prime sources of publications which easily elude the legal deposit net. The Stationery Office publish less than 30 per cent of the total government output, the rest being departmental or sub-departmental publications. Of course the major documents are easy enough to identify and acquire, but items like research reports produced in limited numbers or duplicated departmental circulars present the task not only of identification, but sometimes also of acquisition since the response of the department to a request to deposit can vary quite arbitrarily and from officer to officer. The argument often hinges on what is meant by 'availability to the public'. The governmental publicity leaflet is also elusive, and often there is no alternative but to visit the distribution outlet as though one were a member of the general public. The resultant booty is not worthless: by way of illustration, I recall the case of a researcher who gained valuable information on the Post Office's research and development programmes from this type of source, after he had been thwarted in his direct requests to that intransigent body. This example serves incidentally as an epitome of the confusion which exists generally within government departments and agencies about information which is in the public domain and that which is not.

One conspicuous omission from the existing provision of legal deposit is microform, though it is to be hoped that the next revision of the law will rectify this. Its uses in publication now stretch far beyond the reproduction of the already-published page. It is a convenient way of making available manuscript text, it can be used to present a new arrangement of literature previously scattered (as the Harvester Press have done), it can be a form of output from the computer (COM) as many librarians worried by the cost of maintaining their manual catalogues have discovere and—perhaps most pregnant with possibilities for the future—it can be use to supplement or modify the pattern of printed journal publication. This can take a number of forms. A whole journal may exist in microform, although there are very few examples where there are not corresponding printed journals. There are journals which consist only of abstracts or synopses which are supplemented by the full text in microfiche available on demand (the *Journal of chemical research* from 1977 onwards is such an example). There are the hybrid journals, such as the *Journal of medic history* from 1977, which consist partly of texts of articles fully printed and partly of synopses backed up by on-demand microform. These last two formats are still in the early stages of experiment and it is difficult to assess at present how widespread the practice will become. Of much older vintage is the microform, which is supplementary to a conventionall published journal. It carries mainly the details of scientific research resul such as crystallographic structure data, and is again available on demand, often from a central repository. Finally, there is the imminent prospect of very specialised monographs never being published in the conventional sense but merely being produced as a limited number of masters from which the customer can be supplied with a microform for his retention.

Taken together these advances in the use of microform present acquisition problems for all research libraries. For instance, it may be almost impossible for a serials registration officer to detect a change from the conventional to the hybrid form of publication, unless alerted by a user or a well-informed colleague. However I would suggest that for the natio reference collections the problems are even more acute. The chances of being alerted by a user are considerably less, and in the case of journal titles published in this country the acquisitions system of the national lib has a unique degree of responsibility for gathering all significant research carried out in the world; yet with these changes in the format of scholarly communication it may become unwittingly deficient in worthwhile publications in the public domain which are liable to be requested at some time because they have been cited in other research.

Whatever the effects of the spread of cheap reprography and microfor on the totally comprehensive character of the national printed archive, these could well be dwarfed by the widespread use of on-line, or electron communication between researchers. This is not the place to describe or evaluate in detail the prospects for a 'paperless society' with its personal

140

database, its computer-managed conference, its use of teletext even for domestic purposes, its electronic journal and so on. (12) Yet it is important to emphasise that it is a future which cannot be dismissed as science fiction fantasy. The government-sponsored National Science Foundation in the United States is already supporting the operation and development by the New Jersey Institute of Technology of a test facility for research on electronic information exchange (EIE), and has called for further proposals to test various forms of EIE within small research communities. The main elements in the thesis for this development are economic and technological. On the one hand, the demise of the printed communication, at least in science and technology, will come about because of the increases in the costs of raw materials, labour and energy, and the delays in printing and posting, together with the increasing difficulty in identifying and retrieving scientific information. On the other hand, to quote Senders writing about the electronic journal, 'Scientists exchange ideas proximally by talking and distantly by sending letters. When it became necessary to send letters to relatively large numbers of people, a protojournal came into being. The protojournal still consisted of ideas, but it also acquired a physical nature because it consisted of bundles of paper. In due course, as a result of the need to be able to find the ideas which the paper contained, identification of the bundles by name, and by number and date became necessary. Thus the journal was born. The journal, having acquired a life of its own, continues to exist, although the mechanism for transmitting ideas has altered significantly since its birth with the advent of telecommunications and the computer. 'The journal, then, in its printed bound form has an existence which is unjustified, except as a consequence of habit'. (13)

Admittedly Senders is one of the more ardent advocates of this particular future, and his remarks were confined to scientific and technical information. Such bold views have been qualified by Woodward amongst others who points to the expense of setting up the initial system, and who emphasises that electronic and print systems are not exclusive, since transfer to print can take place for items with proven wide appeal. (14) However we should not allow the central significance of the debate to be obscured by its details: for our purposes the overriding point is that the best-informed experts—irrespective of their stance in the debate, be it radical or temperate —are united in believing that a substantial movement towards electronic information exchange is inevitable. For them it is the speed and the extent of change which is at issue.

Unless all camps are thoroughly confounded and we remain in a print-based research society, the national reference collections will undergo in time a striking metamorphosis. At the moment they can claim fairly to be an adequate if not complete mirror of past and present significant research activity throughout the world, because results have been committed to permanent print. This will not be so in future if the entrails are interpreted correctly, since research workers will be able to interact and communicate the results of their labours to their peer group through an on-line computer network. The physicist, the engineer, the political scientist and the historical demographer will maintain their private databanks as they do now their libraries. 'Publication' will be a decision by the databank's owner to let the results of his work be accessed by others who have been granted their passwords and be transferred to their private databases. The first innovations will be naturally in the disciplines heavily reliant on quantitative data but one cannot exclude the possibility of techniques being evolved at a later date to handle the disciplines more oriented towards subjective judgement such as literary studies; it will depend upon economics as much as upon technical feasibility. Certainly as a more modest variant in the 1990s the text of a learned article stored in machine-readable form on (say) 'Technical innovation in *Hard times*' could be transferred at the push of a button via a telefacsimile link to the 'reader', without the full text necessarily being deposited in a public archive. Although this is deliberately a massive condensation of possible developments (I have said nothing about editorial or refereeing procedure for instance), there is little doubt that the national reference collections will lose their comprehensive archival character unless there is conscious remedial action to ensure that research results displayed on terminals are committed to a more permanent and accessible form. The collections will become arbitrarily selective, even an irrelevant museum of obsolete technology.

Without prejudging the eventual outcome, it is imperative for national libraries to consider and anticipate their actions and reactions. In so doing they will have to address themselves to the large question of what their role is in the advancement of learning. To what extent is it a passive or a positive one? Is there a danger in the era of private databanks and visual display units that the process of scholarly communication will narrow to identified peer groups, forbidding in effect the general random access permissible with a library's printed collections? (They call it browsing.) If this hermetic sealing of research comes about, should the libraries, which now emphasise the need for accessibility and availability, stand in this brave new world lazy by?

In the more immediate and tangible future, the question of how to develop the use of the national reference collections is surely prominent on any agenda. It is a limited view that believes this is a task solely for the librarian fortified by the appropriate user studies. There is an opportunity, both practical and visionary, to foster an active, imaginative partnership between the librarian and his public that has been manifested too rarely in the past, even though it is hardly contentious to say that historically scholarship has been the book. A gradual recognition of the symbiosis proceeds nonetheless, with the recent creation of the 'Center for the Book' at the Library of Congress in the wake of similar ventures in the Hague, Brussels and Paris in which academics, publishers, educationalists as well as librarians are participating and are beginning to confront each other with questions stripped of myth and prejudice. (15) Is it fanciful to see these occasional joint forays grow into an international network?

The questions are there, without doubt. Traditionally national libraries have set great store by published catalogues which took the form of either general but august statements of the library's holdings *in toto* or highly specialised catalogues of particular segments. In both cases the time-scale of production was leisurely, the costs at today's prices prohibitive, and currency was held in comparatively little regard. These grandiose publications until recently represented the major effort of the library to articulate its collections and its role to users. They may have been adequate when the scholarly community was compact, gentlemanly and on the whole equally leisurely, when additional help was not given because it was not desired. Yet these circumstances do not prevail today, and whilst there will always be a place (production costs permitting) for the traditional specialised catalogue more urgent means of communicating the resources of the national library must be found. These resources can be realised, in my view, by adopting modern approaches towards record production and staff deployment.

The bibliographic record should be treated as a tool capable of progressive improvement and extensive manipulation if the library's user is to be served quickly and fully. This is an assumption which is as relevant to the production of retrospective catalogues as it is to the production of current ones. A good example of the new spirit is provided by the British Library's English language eighteenth century short-title catalogue project which it is hoped will be the first phase in an Anglo-American union catalogue undertaking. (16) Such a project had been discussed seriously in bibliographical circles for at least twenty years (17) as the essential conclusion to the charting of English printing, to fill the gap between the short-title catalogues of Pollard and Redgrave and of Wing for the period up to 1700

and the *English catalogue of books* which exists for the nineteenth century.
Yet the sheer volume of printing and the bibliographical niceties in the
eighteenth century had always seemed too daunting. Decades of dedi-
cation would be required. Then in 1977 the British Library announced
its intention, to the astonishment of some purists, to catalogue in three
years all of its unrivalled eighteenth century holdings. To fulfil this commitment a rapid but MARC-compatible method of recording has been
devised and entries will be stored in machine-readable form, ready to be
added to the national database. These techniques will allow the user access to the records by author (more often than not the only point of entry
in previous printed short-title catalogues), title, date, place of publication,
printer and so on. Though exacting standards have been decreed, absolute
perfectionism has been jettisoned for the sake of speed—omissions and over
simplifications where they exist can be corrected later easily enough if the
file is machine-readable. Further worthy of note is the almost embarrass-
ing enthusiasm with which the project has been heralded by eighteenth
century scholars, and because of the time-scale they are more prepared to
cooperate: collaboration need be selfless no longer. Neither is the project
merely a recataloguing exercise, for within six months of its beginning
over 30,000 hitherto individually unrecorded items had been detected.
This has particularly excited the scholars—one distinguished student of
the literature of eighteenth century protest and a lifelong user of the collections was confronted with ninety volumes of radical tracts which had
lain sleeping in the stacks disguised by a thoroughly uninformative collective heading. If national libraries are to discharge their obligations to
their users to the full, such bibliographical aggression must not be dis-
dained.

Turning from the past to the present, national libraries must examine
all possible uses to which their records of current acquisitions may be put
in the steady-state era. Although practice will differ from country to
country, these libraries have to be aware that their acquisitions budgets
are usually at the top of the league, and this fact carries with it corresponding responsibilities. If they wish to be part of a truly national library
service they should consider the most effective and rapid means of adding
the records to the national database so that other libraries may construct
their acquisitions policies with a proper knowledge of those items (especial
expensive ones) which have already been acquired centrally; so that the
national library's records can be used as a basis for local cataloguing; so
that the user may have an accurate conspectus of possible locations; and
so that selective lists of acquisitions—under author, title, language, subjec

etc—may be issued where appropriate to other organisations and individuals. The catalogue of the national reference collections published some years after the period it covers, despite its imposing majesty, must be relegated to a chapter in library history.

The exploitation of the record needs to be matched by an equally vigorous attitude towards staff deployment. The national collections attract professional and academic staff of the highest calibre but have tended to employ them in acquisition and processing tasks at the expense of more overt involvement with the public. Of course a senior specialist knows the 'establishment' scholars in his or her field but with the growth of postgraduate studies there are now many users of the collection who have not yet gained admittance to the club and require guidance or informed insight into the character of that part of the collections which represents their field of study. Otherwise the holdings can appear as a passive and impenetrable enormity; and the benefits of a closer rapprochement may well be mutual since it will allow the library's specialists to monitor more effectively the changing emphases of scholarly endeavour. It is not an accident that at present this comes about most readily in the areas of special collections such as maps, music or government documents where the inevitable anonymity of a large organisation meeting the needs of a multitude of often transient users can be sidestepped. In sum, national libraries which are endowed with a high expertise in their staff should assume a clearer role as a national centre for bibliographic enquiries as part of their total duty to exploit the collections in their custody. Whilst the mechanics of implementing such a policy pose problems, it is in my view equally a question of institutional will.

An underlying theme running throughout this personal credo—if a credo can consist largely of questions—is the desirability of bringing library administrators, scholars, bibliographers, publishers and other interested parties into a more purposeful proximity to each other. It will allow the common problems to be debated and resolved in a unified perspective. Whilst each group may have different emphases and priorities, the library administrator will be more likely to appreciate that his management decisions must be founded on intellectual as well as technical and organisational considerations, to ensure a continuing relevance to the needs of his users; the scholar (18) conversely will be more likely to gain an insight into the often harsh constraints of finance and resource allocation which the pragmatic librarian knows all too well; the bibliographer using the library will have the exciting possibility of working more closely with the libraries' permanent specialists and receiving due library recognition for the value of his labours; and the publisher's participation will permit his own and others' understanding of the complex interrelationship between himself, the author and the text stored in the library for purposes of dissemination to be enlarged.

Of course, some of the questions on the agenda suggested are being or will be tackled by existing groups such as the UGC's Steering Group on Library Research—the nature of browsing, the working patterns of scholar in the humanities are instances. But their concerns are inevitably with academic libraries generally and there is as yet in most countries no well-established 'multi-disciplinary' forum to consider both in theory and in practical detail the changing environment in which the most important single element in the library system, the national library, will operate. It is a forum which has the potential to connect national libraries and their users and allies throughout the developed world. It is a forum that is needed.

REFERENCES

1 A Allardyce and M B Line 'The repository function of the British Library Lending Division' in J W Blackwood (ed) *The future of library collections. Proceedings of a seminar held by the Library Management Research Unit, University of Technology, Loughborough 21-23 March 1977* LMRU report no 7, 1977, 64-69. This is the most detailed expression of the lending division's position, but there are other references to it throughout the proceedings.

2 See for example A Wilson 'The threshold of choice' in *The public library and its users. Proceedings of the Public Libraries Group weekend school, University of Warwick, 25-28 March 1977* LA, Public Libraries Group, 1978. Part of his thesis is that stock control policies should be flexible and carefully monitored, with material which does not meet the demands of the general public being swiftly replaced.

3 This debate is summarised in M B Line 'Storage and deposit libraries' in the forthcoming edition of the *Encyclopedia of library and information science* New York, Dekker.

4 E C Colwell 'Cooperation or suffocation' *College and research libraries* July 1949, 195-198.

5 Allardyce and Line, op cit, 65.

6 Department of Trade *Copyright and designs law. Report of the committee to consider the law on copyright and designs* Cmnd 6732, HMSO, 1977.

7 D N Wood 'Local acquisition and discarding policies in the light of national library resources and services' *Aslib proceedings* 29(1) Januar 1977, 30.

8 D J Urquhart 'The Urquhart report on academic libraries' in J W Blackwood (ed) op cit, 1-9. Urquhart is very dismissive of the value of browsing as an aid to research.

9 J Haller *Lebenserinnerungen; Gesehenes, Gehörtes, Gedachtes* Stuttgart, Kohlhammer, 1960, 236. I am indebted to Professor Bernhard Fabian for this reference.

10 A recent study of the patterns of use of stock acquired by the University of Pittsburg in 1969 is revealing in this respect. *Library journal* 102(13) July 1977, 1438.

11 F W Ratcliffe 'Problems of open access in large academic libraries' *Libri* 18(2) 1968, 95-111.

12 For an extreme view on the prospects for a paperless society, see F W Lancaster 'The dissemination of scientific and technical information' in *Norddata 76* Helsinki, 1976, 1294-1327; and D Bell 'Teletext and technology. New networks of knowledge and information in post-industrial society' *Encounter* June 1977, 9-28, which also deals with this future in a most stimulating and readable fashion.

13 J Senders 'An on-line scientific journal' *The information scientist* 11(1) March 1977, 3-9.

14 A M Woodward *The electronic journal—an assessment* Aslib 1976.

15 The objectives of the Library of Congress Center are put succinctly by Daniel Boorstin in the *Library of Congress information bulletin* 37(3) 20 January 1978, 58.

16 The project is described by R C Alston 'Progress towards an eighteenth century STC: an interim report' *The direction line* (4) autumn 1977, 1-15.

17 R J Roberts 'Towards a short-title catalogue of English eighteenth century books *Journal of librarianship* 2(4) October 1970. 246-262.

18 Although the word 'scholar' is used here in the singular, it should be noted that major research libraries are used increasingly by teams of scholars, often working on projects sponsored by research councils, foundations, etc. This tendency of research towards institutionalism is likely to have a noticeable impact on the way in which libraries organise their services and to improve the communication between them and the sponsoring bodies.

THE CONTRIBUTORS

JOHN DEAN, Collections Maintenance Officer, the Milton S Eisenhower Library, Johns Hopkins University, Baltimore, USA.

PETER DUREY, Librarian of the University of Auckland, New Zealand.

STEPHEN GREEN, of the British Library.

NORMAN HIGHAM, Librarian of Bristol University and Chairman of SCONUL (Standing Conference of National and University Libraries) UK.

JOHN HORACEK, Selection Librarian, La Trobe University, Victoria, Australia.

BERNARD NAYLOR, Librarian of the University of Southampton, England.

COLIN STEELE, the editor, is Deputy Librarian of the Australian National University, Canberra.

ELIZABETH WATSON, Head of the Research and Development Unit, Australian National University Library, Canberra.